CONFEDERATES IN THE TROPICS

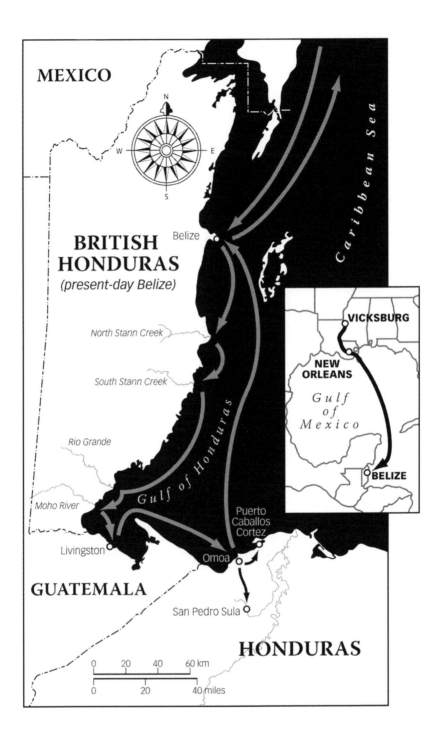

CONFEDERATES
in the
TROPICS

Charles Swett's Travelogue of 1868

Sharon Hartman Strom and Frederick Stirton Weaver

✳

UNIVERSITY PRESS OF MISSISSIPPI

JACKSON

www.upress.state.ms.us

Designed by Peter D. Halverson

The University Press of Mississippi is a member of the Association of American
University Presses.

Map on page ii by Bill Pitts

First printing 2011

∞

Library of Congress Cataloging-in-Publication Data to come

Strom, Sharon Hartman.
Confederates in the tropics : Charles Swett's travelogue of 1868 /
Sharon Hartman Strom and Frederick Stirton Weaver.
p. cm.
Includes bibliographical references and index.
ISBN 978-1-60473-994-7 (cloth : alk. paper) — ISBN 978-1-60473-995-4
(ebook) 1. Swett, Charles, 1828–1910—Travel—Belize. 2. Swett, Charles,
1828–1910—Travel—Honduras. 3. Belize—Description and travel.
4. Honduras—Description and travel. 5. Whites—Southern States—Attitudes—
History—19th century. 6. Southern States—Emigration and immigration—
History—19th century. I. Weaver, Frederick Stirton, 1939– II. Swett, Charles,
1828–1910. A trip to British Honduras and to San Pedro, Republic of Honduras.
III. Title.

F1444.S77 2011
973.8'1—dc22   2010044911

British Library Cataloging-in-Publication Data available

For our mentors and teachers at Cornell University—
David Brion Davis, Tom E. Davis, and Douglas Dowd

✳

And in memory of Cornell alumnus
Michael Henry Schwerner (1939–1964)

Contents

Preface and Acknowledgments

In 2002 the Huntington Library awarded both of us, Sharon Hartman Strom and Frederick Stirton Weaver, Mellon grants, and we spent two months at the library in Pasadena, California, researching U.S. and Central American diplomacy in the Ahmanson Reading Room. We had been hoping to find a way to work together on our mutual interests: mid-nineteenth-century U.S. history, the politics of Central America, and the political economy of slavery and freedom. In the course of looking for materials related to the diplomatic and political career of E. G. Squier, we discovered Charles Swett's 1868 pamphlet, *A Trip to British Honduras and to San Pedro, Republic of Honduras*. We were fascinated by Swett's matter-of-fact, pragmatic description of contemporary life in British and Spanish Honduras and by his themes: the palpable dismay of Southern whites from the consequences of the Civil War and the possibility of Confederates migrating to Central America.

We began an explication of the pamphlet, which had been typeset poorly, had numerous typographical errors and appendixes in Spanish, and was difficult to read in its existing format. Although we located a few copies of Swett's travelogue in other libraries, none of these, unless scanned, a then-laborious process, could be converted to a usable format for word processing, so we set about typing the text into our computers. Swett was a mysterious figure, and the few printed versions of his life, as well as his family's memorabilia, had some glaring lapses—for example, the belief that he had attended West Point and was serving in the U.S. Army as the Civil War began.

On our next trip west from Rhode Island to Pasadena, we stopped in Vicksburg and began a serious inquiry into Swett's life. The building on Washington Street that had housed his family's hardware store was still there, high up on the bluffs overlooking the Mississippi River and the railroad tracks that now line the waterfront. We found helpful aides in the Vicksburg Public Library and much of the useful information that allowed us to fill in the particulars of the lives of the Swett and Oates families in Mississippi. At the Old Court House Museum, we saw the glass showcase exhibit of Swett's Battery, complete with the unit's battle flag and Swett's old uniform. We read Swett's recollections of his artillery unit and looked at the weathered tax roll of 1853, important clues to the status of Charles and his father, Daniel, and their commitment—despite the fact that they were, in essence, New Englanders—to the cause of the Confederacy.

We appreciate the assistance of the past and present staff at the Old Court House Museum: Gordon Cotton, Jeffrey Giambrone, and George Bolan; Huey Purvis of the Warren County Central Records Department; the staff of the Mississippi Historical Society in Jackson; the Reader Services Department at the Huntington Library; the services of the Vicksburg Public Library; and the reference department at the U.S. Military Academy at West Point. We thank in particular scholars Randall Miller, Robert E. May, and Daniel Lewis, who smoothed out some of our rough spots and provided important support when we needed it. Thanks as well to Elwood (Woody) Coleman Jr., Margaret Haas, and Michael Sweet for their invaluable genealogical research and family photographs and their generosity in sharing them with us.

We continue to be grateful readers at the Huntington Library and Botanical Gardens in Pasadena, one of the most delightful places to work (and wander) in the world. The calm and quiet of the Monte Vista Grove retirement community and the assistance of Nancy Lain and Ed Cortez have made our stays in Pasadena pleasant and productive.

CONFEDERATES IN THE TROPICS

Part I

Introduction

✳

THE SWETT FAMILY, RECONSTRUCTION, AND THE
DREAM OF EMIGRATION

In 1868 Charles Swett, a forty-year-old former Confederate from Warren County, Mississippi, published a badly typeset pamphlet of his essay and travelogue, *A Trip to British Honduras and to San Pedro, Republic of Honduras.* Son of a Vicksburg hardware merchant and the owner of a small plantation about six miles east of Vicksburg, Swett owned seventeen slaves until emancipation, served as an officer in an artillery unit during the Civil War, and then participated in Mississippi politics as Reconstruction began.

Charles Swett used the device of a day-by-day diary to describe a trip he had recently taken with "several friends and relatives." These travelers wanted to determine whether British Honduras and Honduras would be suitable sites for establishing expatriate communities of former Confederates hoping to escape from the travails of Radical Reconstruction.[1] Swett's "Prefatory Remarks" to the diary—an opinion piece in the style of a newspaper editorial—are dated October 7, 1867, more than two months before he and his colleagues began their journey, and the purpose of Swett's introduction of less than one page seems to have been to assure readers that he had remained true to his vow to present the diary verbatim.

Swett's "Prefatory Remarks," however, let his readers know that his participation in the trip to Central America did not signal support for the emigration of white Southerners from their Southern homelands. He agreed with Confederate luminaries such as Robert E. Lee, Jefferson Davis, and P. T. Beauregard, who were exhorting whites to stay at home, resist

Northern Reconstruction, and rebuild the Old South.[2] Swett's "Prefatory Remarks" contain both practical and sentimental reasons for staying in the South, but his main goal in publishing the pamphlet was to make accurate and reliable information available to those thinking of leaving. He hoped to counter the inaccurate and exaggerated pro-emigration hyperbole that agents working on commission for foreign governments and private ventures were circulating throughout the South.

Despite the efforts of respected former leaders of the Confederacy, hundreds of thousands of white Southerners left the U.S. South after the Civil War to make new lives elsewhere. Most of these people moved to the U.S. Midwest and West, but others moved north to "Yankeedom" in a much less advertised, often surreptitious migration.[3] In addition to this internal migration, thousands of other white Southerners left the United States with the intention of permanently residing in foreign lands.

Because records are so scattered and incomplete and because so many people returned to the United States, there can be little confidence in numerical estimates. Nevertheless, despite the enthusiasm for emigration expressed in newspapers, diaries, correspondence, and public meetings, a reasonable guess is that only 8,000 to 10,000 white emigrants left the U.S. South for Latin America.[4] Others went to Canada, Europe, Egypt, and Asia. Like those who moved west or north within the United States, these expatriates mostly fled the U.S. South as individuals or families. But most of those who decided to go to Latin America were in better-organized, sizable groups whose leaders hoped to build new communities in order to sustain their identities as white Southerners and preserve what they saw as traditional Southern values and ways of life.[5]

After a brief introduction to the Swett family; the region around Warren County, Mississippi; and the travails of post–Civil War Mississippi, we describe the attempts of former Confederates to settle in Mexico, Brazil, and Venezuela. A more extensive discussion of British Honduras and Honduras follows. The pamphlet itself is reproduced in its entirety, although we have shifted some paragraphs from the appendixes into the diaries to make Swett's descriptions richer and the chronology clearer. Documents in Spanish have been translated into English.

THE SWETT FAMILY OF WARREN COUNTY

Like many other migrants to Mississippi in the 1830s and 1840s, the Swett family came from the North with skills that enabled them to become prosperous and prominent citizens in a thriving new economy based on plantation slavery and river transport. Daniel Swett (1804–1878), the father of Charles Swett, was descended from old Yankee stock from Newbury and Haverhill, Massachusetts, thriving towns outside Boston. Daniel's father was a Revolutionary War veteran, and as a young man Daniel apprenticed as a mechanic in Haverhill, probably acquiring skills in the metal and lumber trades as industrialization took hold in water-powered mills throughout New England.

Along with many New England families in the early nineteenth century, Daniel Swett and his new wife, Sarah Hunt, sought greater economic opportunity by migrating to either the West or the South. In 1827 the couple went to Georgetown, a community in the District of Columbia west of the new capital of the United States, where Daniel plied his trade as a mechanic, the nineteenth-century's version of an engineer, perhaps working on projects for the federal government.

Charles Swett was born in Georgetown in 1828, and when he was eight years old Daniel and Sarah moved their growing family to Vicksburg, Mississippi. The city, the seat of Warren County, is on the Mississippi River and adjacent to where the Yazoo River feeds into the Mississippi River, the southernmost point of the Yazoo-Mississippi Delta. Warren County is also at the northern point of what is known as the Natchez District—an eight-county unit bordering both sides of the Mississippi. The fertility of the alluvial soil, the density of large plantations, and the great wealth of the planters in slaves and productive land made the district unusual, if not unique, in the South.[6]

When the Swetts arrived in the mid-1830s, the Delta region north of Warren County was a raw frontier that had been opened to white settlers only since 1832, when the U.S. government forcefully relocated the Chickasaw and Choctaw residents to Indian Territory (Oklahoma). But the outlines of the Mississippi Delta, particularly in Natchez County, were clear. There was a glut of slaves on the eastern seaboard, and many young white adults on the Mississippi frontier were children of eastern slave owners who had either inherited slave property or capital derived from plantation profits. Northern migrants with investment capital joined them in creating a new and powerful slaveholding regime. The horrific internal slave trade between the Old South and the western frontier provided aspiring planters in Mississippi with 100,000 slaves to clear the dense vegetation of the malaria-infested swamps, drain the potentially rich land, and grow cotton, now in great demand in both New England and Britain. Slaves soon constituted 80 percent of the Mississippi Delta's population.[7] Draconian slave codes gave white planters life-and-death control over African Americans in the Delta. The grandchildren of these frontier families who thought about resettling elsewhere in the Americas after the Civil War would have none of these advantages in labor, racial policy, and market demand for their agricultural products.

Plantation construction and cotton cultivation required large inventories of tools and equipment, and Daniel Swett opened a hardware store in the mid-1830s on the bluffs overlooking the Vicksburg Mississippi River landing that soon became the most successful and widely used such enterprise in the Vicksburg region. The Swetts also purchased farmland four miles east in Warren County. Daniel Swett's nine slaves divided their labor between the Swett hardware store and the Warren County estate. Swett, unlike many of his Warren County neighbors, was not a large-scale plantation owner; he earned most of his considerable livelihood from his store.

Situated about halfway between New Orleans and Memphis on the Mississippi River, Vicksburg was a major port and a vital link in the flow of goods and people, including slaves, connected via river traffic to the Gulf of Mexico, the Ohio and the Missouri rivers, the Great Lakes, and the Erie Canal. An advertisement on the back of the *1866 Vicksburg Mississippi Directory* announced that Swett's store sold "Hardware, Guns, Caps, Plantation and Garden Implements, Carpenters and Smiths Tools, French Crockery & China, Glassware, Oil and Lamps, Wood and Basket Ware, Wallpaper, Manila and Cotton Rope, Landreth's Garden Seed, &c." The Warren County tax roll of 1853 showed that Daniel paid a state tax of $110 on the $57,000 worth of merchandise he had sold that year; he owned a piano and five clocks as well as his nine slaves. The family attended the Presbyterian Church and, like many others in Vicksburg, preferred the Whig Party. The majority of the white male voters of Vicksburg, hoping to avoid the economic disruption of a civil war and to preserve slavery, supported John Bell of the Constitutional Union Party in the 1860 U.S. presidential election.[8]

Charles Swett spent his boyhood in Vicksburg in the combined family store and residence on Washington Street, Vicksburg's most important commercial avenue. Five of Charles's ten siblings died in childhood or early adulthood, a common occurrence in the unhealthy environment of life along the river, where yellow fever epidemics were common. As the oldest son in a large and growing family, Charles worked alongside his father and other male clerks, acquiring the retail and artisan skills required of a nineteenth-century mechanic and business owner, including those of surveying.[9] As for retailing, he would say in his pamphlet, "if you lived in

1. Vicksburg, Mississippi, levee and steamboats, 1864. Library of Congress Prints and Photographs Division, Washington, D.C., http://www.loc.gov/pictures/resource/cwpb.01012/, accessed June 15, 2009.

the United States you would think slavery still in existence, as with us there is certainly no class of men who are worked harder than the merchants" (British Honduras: insert within January 6 entry).

Swett's allegiance to the Old South that he claimed was being destroyed in 1867 had been amplified by his marriage. In 1851 he wed Susan Amanda Oates, daughter of Jacob Oates, a planter who had migrated to Warren County from Georgia with his wife, Susan Temperance Bonner, born in Massachusetts. The Oates family census tally (of whites) of 1850 included an overseer, indicative of the large capital that the Oates family had invested in African American slaves. Amanda had been born in Mississippi, and the newlywed couple acquired farmland adjacent to Amanda's parents' plantation.

By 1853 Amanda and Charles owned twelve slaves, and it is likely that Charles's father-in-law, Jacob, helped Amanda manage his affairs while Charles was away for the four long bleak years of the bloodiest conflict in U.S. history. Amanda had considerable domestic duties; she would give birth to eight children between 1852 and 1876. Given her close ties to her family and to the place where she had grown up, it seems unlikely she would have been enthusiastic about a move to British Honduras or Spanish Honduras, where diseases of various kinds were a constant threat to all, especially infants, even more so than in Mississippi.

The coming of secession and civil war in 1861 changed the family's lives immediately. As the community responded to the 1860 election of Abraham Lincoln, the governor of Mississippi convened a constitutional convention in January 1861, and Warren County's white men elected two delegates for the convention.[10] Although Jefferson Davis and his brother had adjoining plantations twenty miles south of Vicksburg in Warren County, the Warren County delegates were initially against secession.

One of the Warren County delegates, Walter Brooke, after trying to slow down the rush to secession, vainly proposed holding a statewide referendum. After that was defeated, he became one of the eighty-four who voted for leaving the Union, explaining that he thought there were more desirable alternatives but that secession was preferable to doing nothing. The other Warren County delegate, Thomas A. Marshall, voted with the fifteen who were against secession, and from this point, Brooke and Marshall were usually on opposing sides.[11] Brooke was elected by the convention to be a Mississippi delegate to the Montgomery (or Southern/Secession) Convention, which had representatives from South Carolina, Georgia, Florida, Alabama, Mississippi, and Louisiana. The purpose of the convention was to establish a provisional government of the states that had already seceded until a formal confederation could be formed, but the provisional government was not intended to last more than a year. Some of the resistance to secession came from planters who argued that secession was likely to lead to war, slave revolts, defeat, and the end of slavery. At worst, if emancipation were to prevail through the political process, it would likely be gradual and with compensation for lost property in slaves.[12]

When the war began in April 1861, slaveholders, despite their misgivings about secession, rallied to the Confederate States of America (CSA), and Charles Swett set about raising a cavalry company. The governor of Mississippi thought that Mississippi already had too many cavalry units and asked Swett to form an artillery company. Swett agreed to do so; after all, he had considerable experience with machinery and firearms through the hardware business. The Mississippi state government supplied four cannons, caissons, carriages, and forge, and Warren County residents provided the horses, uniforms, supplies, and a flag. Swett raised the Warren County Light Artillery (known ever after as "Swett's Battery"), which included two of Swett's brothers, William and Daniel, and the husband of Swett's sister, Thomas Havern, who had worked in the Swett hardware business alongside Charles, William, and the two Daniels.[13]

The newly formed battery assembled on Daniel Swett's Sr.'s plantation and voted Charles Swett captain and leader of the unit. A friend of the Swett family asked the battery to join the Army of Kentucky, and since the Mississippi governor was not in Jackson, the arrangement was approved by the state adjutant general. When the governor returned, he was angry and insisted the battery, outfitted in good part by the state, return to Mississippi. By that time, however, the battery and its equipment were on a steamer headed to the headquarters of the Army of Kentucky (soon merged into the Army of Tennessee).

Swett and Swett's Battery served with distinction.[14] Some of the reasons for the battery's later praise are evident in Swett's 1908 chronicle of its battles. Swett, in a rare moment of puffery, said that "Swett's Battery prided itself on always being ready for whatever was to be done." Some of this success was no doubt due to Swett's mechanical knowledge, and his interest in the modern art of technological invention is hinted at here:[15]

> Our two wood workers were not only finished carpenters, but could do anything in wood that was ever placed before them, but our horse shoer, who learned his trade in New York, had a poor idea of general black-smith work. What pursuit can a man follow successfully, who has comparatively no mechanical ideas? . . . There are men who can do very fine work at their chosen trade when they have everything necessary to do with, but give them a broad-axe, hand saw, jack knife and a cord of wood, and they would never make a model of a steam engine, as some whittlers have done. Oh! For the everlasting fitness of things!

Swett's Battery fought in some of the most gut-wrenching battles of the Civil War: Shiloh, Chattanooga, Chicamauga, Lookout Mountain, and Missionary Ridge. The losses of men rose steadily. Swett's two brothers survived, but his brother-in-law, Thomas Havern, died at Chattanooga. Although Swett had declined several offers of promotion to major, probably because of his tendency toward personal modesty and his reluctance to leave his men, he did follow an order to serve as inspector general of artillery for the Army of Tennessee in mid-1864. To his eternal regret, he was not with his Mississippi soldiers three months later when they were decimated by Sherman's troops in the Battle of Jonesboro south of Atlanta in 1864. Years later he was able to list the names of every man who had served under his command and where and how each man's wound and death occurred.

Swett's extravagant language in his "Prefatory Remarks" must be understood in light of the losses of his beloved battery: "Should we not remain here and keep forever green the graves of departed heroes, or should we desert a land that has been bought at such a price, and forget the suffering and privation of those who are now beyond reach of our sympathy . . . but whose memories we should cherish, and whose deeds we should keep forever fresh in our memories?"

The Siege and Occupation of Vicksburg

Vicksburg, the seat of Warren County, is located on high bluffs above the Mississippi River. Both sides recognized early in the war that control of this "Gibraltar of the Confederacy" was essential. Once New Orleans, Natchez, and Memphis had been taken by Union forces in 1862, Vicksburg remained a major obstacle to Union control of the entire Mississippi River valley and the Union's ability to cut off Confederate supply routes through Mexico, Texas, Arkansas, and northern Louisiana.[16]

General Ulysses S. Grant poured thousands of troops into the region, bombarding Vicksburg and sending countless men into assaults on the bluffs overlooking the river. After the lengthy and destructive siege, Union forces captured Vicksburg and its immediate environs on July 4, 1863, and controlled Vicksburg and most of Warren County through the second half of the Civil War. An African American regiment was critically important in taking Vicksburg, and the entire siege ended with 17,000 Union soldiers' deaths; only 4,000 of them were ever identified. Vicksburg fell on the same Fourth of July that saw Lee's retreat from Gettysburg.

Confederate deaths in the siege of Vicksburg totaled 1,600, a fraction of those suffered by Union troops. But the effect of the siege—and the war—on the civilian population was dire. During the Civil War, most able-bodied white men were away in the army, and women and children often managed farms, plantations, and businesses. They faced unruly black workers and servants and marauding soldiers from both armies. The Swett and Oates plantations were in the direct path of retreating Johnny Rebs and Grant's advancing armies coming west from Jackson to Vicksburg. Soldiers living off the land stole and destroyed property including clothing, furniture, livestock, and crops. Attempts to hide the family silver were usually in vain. Fears of black uprisings and of sexual assaults against white women were commonplace.[17]

Despite widespread unease about secession, once the decision was made the white population of Vicksburg rallied to the cause, and the terrible devastation of the siege of Vicksburg further alienated local whites from the

Union cause and its army of occupation from the middle of July 1863 to the end of the war in 1865. Local white women were frequently arrested and occasionally banished for showing disrespect for the United States and for smuggling mail and goods to the Confederate side of the lines. Elizabeth Eggleston was indicted for a number of such offences, and after the war she was the founding president of the Vicksburg Confederate Cemetery Association.[18]

The white population of occupied Vicksburg especially resented and feared the thousands of African Americans who left plantations still in Confederate-held areas and went to Union-held Vicksburg to escape slavery. The city was besieged by transients. In 1860, 4,500 people lived in Vicksburg, nearly a third of them slaves, and only a handful of free black men and women. By the end of 1865 the city's population reached 15,000, over half of them recently freed women, children, and men. The overwhelming presence of African Americans made the white population nervous at best, and rumors of an imminent black insurrection circulated constantly. The presence of uniformed and armed black soldiers was especially unnerving to whites, and as a concession to them, President Andrew Johnson, on March 22, 1866, ordered all black troops mustered out of the army despite their significant contributions to Union victories at Vicksburg and elsewhere.[19] Figure 2 is a picture of the kinds of troops that made whites in Vicksburg so uneasy.

Celebrations of the Fourth of July by blacks and whites evolved in different ways. Some Vicksburg whites refused to celebrate the holiday for decades. African Americans celebrated the Fourth with enthusiasm in segregated ceremonies that often included readings of the Declaration of Independence and the Thirteenth, Fourteenth, and Fifteenth amendments.[20]

Charles Swett had suffered terrible personal and property losses in the war, losses that the Union celebration of the Fourth of July made more poignant. His farm was only a few miles away from what would be designated a national cemetery in 1867 and the Vicksburg Military Park in 1895. His home, his city, and his state—and then with reunion, his country—had become, literally, tragic and sacred ground. Abandoning this ground was tantamount to treason for him. Nonetheless, he understood fully that white Southerners were experiencing hard times and were in a deep state of emotional shock. He knew that there was a strong attraction to the idea of leaving the U.S. South and going abroad. Indeed, his "Prefatory Remarks" constitute a catalog of ills both economic and psychic, and they have a shrill tone that is very different from the rest of the diaries, letting us know that he was as demoralized as anyone in the state and might even consider leaving under the right circumstances.

2. District of Columbia. Company E, 4th U.S. Colored Infantry, at Fort Lincoln, between 1863 and 1866. Library of Congress Prints and Photographs Division, Washington, D.C., http://www.loc.gov/pictures/item/cwp2003000946/PP/, accessed July 1, 2010.

PRESIDENTIAL AND CONGRESSIONAL RECONSTRUCTION

In the years after the war, Southern whites struggled to regain political control in the Deep South. The principal threat to white political dominance was neither Union troops nor African American violence but rather the potential of African American politics. If black men were to gain the franchise, elections throughout former Confederate states would be fraught with dangers for white control of state and local government. In the late 1860s African Americans were majorities of the populations in Mississippi, South Carolina, and Louisiana and only slightly less than half the populations of Florida, Georgia, and Alabama.[21]

Under the terms of an easygoing Presidential Reconstruction of 1865 and 1866, these potential black voting blocs were not a problem, because whites simply prevented the freedmen from registering and voting. Andrew Johnson had become president of the United States when Confederate supporters assassinated Abraham Lincoln five days after General Robert E. Lee surrendered at Appomattox, but even with a Southern sympathizer in the White House, Southern white politics after the war did not immediately return to antebellum patterns. Congress had other ideas. As conditions of being readmitted to the Union and having their congressional delegations seated in the U.S. Senate and House of Representatives, the federal government required the states in the Confederacy to convene constitutional conventions to declare the secession proclamations null and void and to outlaw slavery. Radical Republicans were soon determined to give the vote to black men.[22]

The all-white male constituency of Warren County elected Charles Swett to be one of the two Warren County representatives at the constitutional convention that convened in Jackson on August 14, 1865. According to the convention's official journal, the convention leadership appointed Swett to no committees, and there is no record of his contributing to the ten days of debate. He did, however, vote regularly, usually with Thomas A. Marshall, the second delegate from Warren County. Marshall, a lawyer from Vicksburg and, like Swett, a Whig, was the Warren County delegate to the 1861 convention who had voted against seceding from the United States. Marshall and Swett were increasingly in the minority in their voting in the 1865 convention, but since so many debates and votes were about specific wordings and tactics, it is difficult to be sure of their overall sentiments.[23]

Since Mississippi's constitutional convention was the first such convention after the war, Andrew Johnson paid close attention to its deliberations in the hopes that the convention could be a model for his vision of Reconstruction throughout the South. In a dispatch read to the convention's opening session, President Johnson assured the delegates that without nullifying the secession declaration and explicitly outlawing slavery, there was no chance that Mississippi's U.S. representatives and senators would be seated in Washington, D.C. He then added:

> If you could extend the elective franchise to all persons of color who own real estate valued at not less than $250 and pay taxes thereon, you would completely disarm the adversary and set an example the other states will follow. This you can do with perfect safety, and you thus place the southern States, in reference to free persons of color, upon the same basis with the free states. I hope and trust your convention will do this and, as a consequence, the radicals, who are wild upon negro franchise, will be completely foiled in their attempt to

keep the States from renewing their relations to the Union by not ac-
cepting their senators and representatives.[24]

The convention adjourned after nullifying the secession proclamation,
declaring slavery illegal, organizing the state and local judiciary, and setting a date for the next election—October 2, 1865. But they ignored President Johnson's cynical ploy of granting the franchise to African Americans
who satisfied a property qualification not required of white voters. In the
months after the war, the terror of any hint of enfranchising black men
so permeated the convention that opening the door even a crack was too
threatening. The unwillingness of the delegates to discuss racial issues was
also illustrated when a delegate from Marshall County proposed that "a
judicious system of *colonization* should be adopted" to deal with the "re-
dundant population of freedmen." The resolution was "indefinitely post-
poned" with no debate. On the other hand, delegates' occasional strong
criticisms of the 1861 decision to secede and of the institution of slavery are
striking.[25]

In October Mississippi white men chose state legislators, a governor, and
U.S. representatives and senators. The Warren County constituency elected
Charles Swett to the state senate. His election indicated his stature among
Warren County whites, despite his diffidence, and the *Daily Vicksburg Herald* of April 3, 1867, again illustrated local eminent white men's high regard
for Swett. The newspaper reprinted ten letters dated between March 27
and 30, 1867, about a duel being planned by two prominent newspapermen.
Charles Swett was one of the four who offered to serve as disinterested mediators between the aggrieved parties. Of the nine men eventually involved
in the successful resolution of the dispute, all were identified as colonels
and generals except for Swett, who was still "Major Swett."[26]

In late 1865 the first postwar Mississippi state legislature passed a series of laws regarding contracts, apprenticeships, debt, and vagrancy that
severely restricted African Americans' freedoms. These laws, collectively
known as the Black Codes, became common throughout the former Confederate states, where local whites were beginning to assume control over
state affairs with the support of President Johnson. Nevertheless, the U.S.
Congress continued to deny seats to the representatives of the former Confederate states between 1865 and 1868, except for Tennessee, which quickly
satisfied all of the conditions for readmission to the Union and was readmitted in July 1866.

The November 1866 national elections were a serious setback for white
Southerners trying to reestablish political control in the South. They

brought strong, veto-proof Republican majorities to both the U.S. House of Representatives and the U.S. Senate. The new Congress, over presidential vetoes, supplanted Andrew Johnson's mild Presidential Reconstruction with the much harsher Congressional Reconstruction in March and July 1867. Congress established martial law in ten Southern states, enfranchised black men in former Confederate states only, and laid the groundwork for abolishing the Black Codes by dissolving the all-white state legislatures that had created them. The hopes of those Southerners anticipating a prompt withdrawal of federal troops and termination of the Freedman's Bureau were crushed.[27]

The new Reconstruction acts led to yet another constitutional convention in Mississippi. But high rates of black voter registration and the temporary disenfranchisement of some categories of former Confederates made African Americans a majority of the Mississippi electorate. It seemed likely that Mississippi white men would lose the November 1867 election for delegates to the state's constitutional convention, and their response in Mississippi as a whole, including Warren County, was to boycott the election. By doing so, they believed that they could stall the constitutional convention and the entire process of Congressional Reconstruction. Whites constituted fewer than a quarter of Warren County's more than 6,000 total registered voters, and it was reported that only about eight white voters cast ballots in the election. In Warren County, and throughout the South, the whites' strategy enabled black constituencies to elect their own representatives to the convention without challenge. While blacks made up about 20 percent of those elected to the constitutional convention, the majority of the Mississippi convention delegates were white "carpetbaggers" and "scalawags" in favor of Reconstruction and blacks' civil rights.[28] Charles Swett was not elected again as a delegate from Warren County.

As Swett wrote his "Prefatory Remarks" in 1867, it looked as though the postwar project of the traditional white leadership's attempts to reclaim a hold on political power in Mississippi was in serious jeopardy. No doubt Swett's personal involvement with the canceled 1865 constitution and losing his seat in the state senate made it especially hard on him and lay behind the bitter words: "We are politically nothing . . . the party in power striving by every means in its power to place an inferior race in a position of political importance."

Swett's fear that African Americans might govern whites was well-founded, and there was an outstanding example close to home. Former Confederates were dismayed as they watched the career of Hiram Rhoades Revels unfold in the heart of the Mississippi Delta. Revels was a college-educated

3. Hiram Revels (1827–1901), between 1860 and 1875. Library of Congress Prints and Photographs Division, Washington, D.C., http://www.loc.gov/pictures/item/brh2003001200/PP/, accessed July 8, 2010.

minister who had organized two black regiments and accompanied one of them to Vicksburg during the siege of 1863. He returned to Mississippi in 1866 with his growing family to serve as pastor of the Natchez African Methodist Episcopal Church and to organize schools for black children. Newly enfranchised black voters elected him alderman in 1868 and then representative of Adams County to the Mississippi State Senate in 1869. That body elected Revels one of Mississippi's two senators, making him the first person of color ever to serve in the U.S. Senate.[29]

Although Charles Swett was writing from a particular locale and despite the unique wartime experience of Warren County, he presumed to speak for "the better class" of Southerners in general. He believed that his view was true for the planter class, whites who identified with them, and those who longed for white supremacy throughout the South. Swett looked to the planters and the Confederate elite, nearly one and the same, as the backbone of everything important in the South, and there is no question that in spite of the devastation of the war, this class continued to be the most articulate stratum of Southern society, possessed the greatest economic resources, and was still overrepresented in Southern white leadership.

The political plight of Charles Swett and his colleagues was grim, and Swett's most emotionally expressed lamentation in his "Prefatory Remarks" was over the social and political consequences of black equality. Here he indulges in the most extreme imagery and expresses the greatest despair. If white abasement continued indefinitely, he could not object to deserting the beloved homeland. But first a valiant struggle to restore the old racial order must be mounted. He would shift to a more neutral tone in the rest of the pamphlet, a stance more in keeping with his commitment to being a dispassionate recorder for those considering emigration—but the change in his tone is abrupt.

Economic Doldrums

Swett also devoted several pages in his "Prefatory Remarks" to the economic situation in Mississippi, which was indeed dismal for nearly everyone. A few Southerners did well from the war, including Charles Swett's father, Daniel, in the hardware business. But the war was an economic disaster for the majority of the region's rich and powerful planters, whether they fought in the Confederate army or stayed on their plantations. All through the war their highly visible estates were particularly susceptible to looting and destruction by passing Federal and Confederate armies, black and white refugees, and Confederate deserters and demobilized soldiers on their way home.[30]

Swett's own economic situation was dire. The 1870 net worth of his property in Warren County was less than a quarter of what it had been in 1860. He had lost the value of seventeen slaves, and in an additional disaster in 1866, his house burned down along with several others in the neighborhood, perhaps cases of arson.[31] He was not, however, as devastated as some; the plantation elite in Warren County had owned hundreds of slaves and depended almost entirely on cotton for income. Because of Daniel Swett's prosperous hardware store, the Swett men's skills in the mechanical trades were another source of income in what would be a new Southern economy built on textile mills, railroad construction, and lumbering.

Southern planters had few financial resources with which to bring their properties back to previous levels of production. The physical destruction of plantations and the uncompensated manumission of over 3,500,000 slaves—roughly 45 percent of the value of planters' antebellum property—nearly bankrupted the old elite. Confederate dollars and bonds were worthless. During the last years of the war, desperate state governments squeezed all resources within reach, and federal officials levied high taxes on real property.[32] Planters' holds on their plantations were precarious.

There were a few examples of Union forces expropriating and redistributing large estates during the war, with the best-known examples in the Georgia Sea Islands and Missouri. General William Tecumseh Sherman attempted the most extensive redistribution of land. He granted 20,000 freed slaves an average of fifty acres apiece of former plantation land between Jacksonville, Florida, and Charleston, South Carolina. Federal authorities, however, quickly reversed the reforms.[33]

Despite some agitation in the North for land reform and continuing anxiety by planters about confiscations, land reform was never a formal part of postwar Reconstruction policies at either the state or federal level. (Several of the states' Congressional Reconstruction constitutional conventions discussed the appropriation of land but did not draft legislation for it.) Federal authorities usually returned confiscated land, and antebellum landowning patterns changed little in the first few decades after the war, although there was some turnover in ownership as more African Americans and Northerners began to purchase land.[34]

The fundamental insecurity of planter property stemmed from a more mundane cause. Like most agriculturists, Southern planters depended heavily on credit; they borrowed to prepare for the next crop cycle and repaid the loans when the crop was sold. During the war, however, the Union blockade of Southern shipping and the lack of security prevented most planters from rolling over their debt for several years. As a result, both the accumulation of debt principal and unpaid interest created large debts for the planters when the war ended in 1865, and as slaves had frequently been used as collateral, manumission meant that the plantations themselves were exposed to foreclosure.

Regional banks and cotton brokers were also in crisis, which forced many of them to sell off planters' debts to people and institutions outside the South in order to have any chance of remaining solvent. Local debt holders as well as Northern opportunists and institutions foreclosed some plantations, creating turnover of the personnel in the planter class and adding to the weakness of the post–Civil War planter aristocracy. Even for those who kept their plantations, the looming threat of foreclosure and consequent insecurity further undermined planters' hold on Southern politics and culture.

New statewide property taxes were hard on all farmers, large and small, and small farms that had lost much of their male workforce to the army during the war were also deeply in debt. As a result, most states' new constitutions provided some form of debt protection through homestead provisions that exempted a certain value of personal and real property from creditors' reach. But some Natchez District planters did forfeit their plantations for nonpayment of taxes.[35]

Most of the district's indebted planters had serious difficulties in affording the costs of preparing for a new planting season, since their usual sources of lending had liquidity problems. Planters, moreover, were not used to dealing with free wage-earning workers and were reluctant to treat them as such. But cotton prices were high in 1865, and the Natchez District was particularly attractive to prosperous Northern individuals and firms, and they came south in large numbers to lease plantations and open retail stores. In 1865 a majority of the district planters who owned the great estates bordering the Mississippi River, as well as many others back from the river, leased their plantations to Northerners on favorable terms. The crop in 1866, however, was almost completely destroyed by floods and swarms of armyworms.[36] Cotton prices remained high, and some Northern lessees came back the next year, believing that the 1866 disasters were isolated episodes and could lead to lower rents. Floods and armyworms again devastated the district in 1867, and, compounding problems, cotton prices declined by more than 50 percent through the year.[37]

This is the background to Charles Swett's complaint about agricultural production in his "Prefatory Remarks": "loss has attended nearly every effort to produce [cotton] by our own people who were acquainted with the plant, and a like want of success has attended the trials made by those who have come from other sections, and who knew but little of its cultivation, and whose capital was the only advantage they possessed over us."

Lessees from the North did have capital, but they had less after their foray into Mississippi cotton farming. While they were used to working with wage-earning workers, they were not used to working with workers who had vivid memories of slavery and resented most aspects of the old system of labor.

The irony for the old planter class was that by leasing their land, they not only made money, they also avoided going bankrupt in the terrible years for cotton growing right after the war. The postwar agricultural depression itself produced some protection for stressed planters: property prices declined so precipitously that it was not very worthwhile for creditors and tax authorities to foreclose and auction off plantations, and a number of planters in the district managed to pay off enough of their debts to save their plantations within what amounted to an unintended two- or three-year grace period.[38]

The dreary prospects of Southern agriculture prompted Charles Swett to express dissatisfaction with the South's "having been almost entirely engaged in planting, and but comparatively little in manufacturing, and show plainly how poor we have become as a people." He was prescient in voicing an aspect of what would be known later as the credo of the "New South," and probably his experience as an artillery and administrative officer during the Civil War and his father's success in promoting manufactured goods produced in the North underlined for him the handicaps of an agrarian region fighting and then competing with an industrialized one.

The paradox of this is that where industrial and commercial growth was successful in the postwar U.S. South, it produced new business-oriented elites who contributed further to the eclipse of the planter class's power and authority, even as these new elites romanticized and glorified the plantation and Confederate past and lamented the demise of the old racial order.[39] Charles Swett, who was not a typical planter and earned most of his income from a hardware store, exemplified this ambivalence.

He again identified with the antebellum planter class when he wrote, "We are deprived of our former labor system, that enabled us to increase our worldly possessions and enrich the North, and are now compelled to depend upon a system of labor that prevents the possibility of our raising our great staple productions at a price that will prove remunerating." The freeing of slaves was an enormous blow to the very foundation of plantations' productive organization and the region's social system. Slaves had rejected the Confederate cause en mass by crossing enemy lines and serving as laborers and soldiers for the Union army, and planters often expressed deep disappointment at this so-called betrayal when former slaves left their plantations as soon as they could.[40]

Unable to leave the region, most ex-slaves found employment on plantations, although a surprisingly large number quickly moved toward landholding themselves. Efforts to employ an agricultural wage-labor force of freedmen were seldom successful in cotton, because without the threat of physical coercion, freedmen would not acquiesce to the rigors of the gang-labor system, paltry wages, and overseers' humiliations.[41] It was only a few years later that tenant farming and sharecropping became dominant in cotton production as a sort of workable compromise, although sharecropping and renting gave planters less direct control over black labor than they desired and allowed less independence to free blacks than owning land would have. Planters had to make the transition from lord to landlord and from master to employer, and while slavery bound the planter class together, competition among planters for free labor divided them. It was a new world.[42]

But beyond its effects on production, the abolition of slavery destroyed the structure of social control that underlay white supremacy. A surprising omission in Swett's account is any expression of worry about personal security, an anxiety that seemed to permeate much of the white Southern elite after the Civil War. The weakness of the formerly powerful planters and the restiveness of the formerly oppressed majority, poor whites and especially blacks, seemed a serious menace. Secession itself triggered fears of slave revolts, enhanced by Lincoln's Proclamation of Emancipation, declared in September 1862 and put into effect on January 1, 1863. And legislative attempts to restore whites' control over blacks were frustrated when Congressional Reconstruction nullified the Black Codes. The idea of a free black population posed problems for whites, problems with no easy resolution.

The *Vicksburg Daily Herald* ran few stories about local African Americans, and the ones that were reported fell into one of two categories. The most frequent type were lurid stories of blacks thieving, setting fires, murdering whites, breaking out of jail, and other such misbehavior. This category was topped off by an editorial in 1867 vigorously defending white mobs and police in New Orleans, arguing that those who engaged in brutal attacks on African Americans (including lynching and rape) had done so to "prevent a black rebellion." The second kind of reporting about local blacks were stories about black citizens who had supposedly spoken out against Reconstruction or who favored restoring white political privileges.[43]

In Swett's narrative, what we get in place of fear is indignation against "the humiliating fact of equality of races existing among us—when an inferior holds public position, and even serves in the capacity of representatives of the people." In his rant, he was surprisingly easy on Union occupiers and even more so on local blacks except (and it is a *large* exception) that they were in combination destroying the racial hierarchy that he saw to be natural, just, and the intention of the Creator.

Social and political threats to white Southern elites in the postwar era, however, did not only come from African Americans and Northern busybodies. Swett's exclusive focus on race and the fear of black equality was a common strategy among Southern elites to contain nonslaveholding whites, whom they held in profound contempt but needed to control.[44] The white Southern leadership was hostile to universal white male suffrage, and its termination was to be on the agenda after the South achieved independence as the CSA and beyond. The legislation passed by the Southern states after 1890 aimed at disenfranchising African Americans was based on literacy, property holding, and the payment of poll taxes, and also reduced the number of voters among poor whites. This class exclusion was occasionally mentioned in debates as an attractive feature, but for obvious political reasons, could not be presented openly as a deliberate goal.[45]

After their initial enthusiasm for the war, nonslaveholding white farmers soon became resentful of the unequal apportioning of the war's burden, an unfairness that included multiple avenues for wealthy slaveholders and their sons to evade conscription as well as the inequitable tax system and inflation that financed the Confederacy. They registered this discontent in massive desertions from the Confederate armies, armies that declined in numbers from as early as the first months of 1863. The emancipation of slaves in Union-controlled areas and the large numbers of Southern white men who left families to fight the war also disrupted already contested gender relationships in white Southern households. The guerrilla campaigns Southern rural whites waged against the Confederacy during the Civil War were but the most extreme expression of this general disaffection that historians have called the South's "inner Civil War."[46]

Altogether, planters believed that they could not count on federal authorities to protect them and their property from the anger of former slaves, the resentment of poor whites who believed that the planter class had betrayed their trust during the war that cost them so dearly, and the avarice of Northern carpetbaggers and the perfidy of Southern scalawags. One response by whites was the Ku Klux Klan (KKK), formed by former Confederate officers shortly after the end of the war as a social club, which grew quickly and turned into a terrorist organization in which prosperous men led poor whites in a common cause. Instead of conducting a guerrilla war against armed federal troops, they rode in large numbers at night, garbed in bizarre costumes, including women's dresses, their identities concealed behind masks, hoods, and blackface, and attacked primarily black families with threats, beatings, and killings.[47] The KKK, like the Knights of the Camellia, the White League, the Regulators, the White Line, and similar organizations, was a paramilitary arm of the movement Southern whites called "Redemption"—reestablishing white supremacy. In addition to terrorizing black families, these Redeemers also targeted carpetbaggers and scalawags prominent in state and local governments and blamed them for corruption, extravagance, and high taxes.

Charles Swett does not mention the explicit possibility of using vigilante-style violence to restore white supremacy, and we do not know whether he would have approved of it. The KKK was not active in Mississippi until 1869, when the hooded riders operated mostly in the state's northeastern and eastern counties. While desiring to prevent blacks from becoming prosperous and from voting, the Mississippi KKK distinguished itself from other states' KKKs by a strong emphasis on destroying public schools and intimidating blacks and whites involved in establishing a statewide public school system, although the schools were racially segregated.[48] Of the eleven seceding states, only North Carolina had an antebellum statewide public school system.

Given the time and place in which Charles Swett wrote the "Prefatory Remarks," it is no wonder that he was so morose, acknowledging what he considered valid and genuine reasons underlying whites' desires to emigrate from the South. From his vantage point of 1868, it was impossible to foresee how politically effective the widespread use of white violence against blacks would be. The political resurgence of Southern whites and the accompanying violence against blacks in the 1870s would force blacks to contemplate leaving the South. But in the years immediately after the Civil War, despite appeals for loyal Southerners to stay in the South, it was the whites who left the South—thousands not only moved into the West and Northeast, thousands more went to Latin America to establish expatriate communities.

MEXICO, BRAZIL, AND VENEZUELA

The initial white flight to Mexico was precipitate and poorly organized, an exception to the Confederates' generally orderly emigration to Latin America. Large numbers of Confederates poured over the Mexican border from Texas in a rush following General Robert E. Lee's surrender at Appomattox on April 9, 1865, and General Edmund Kirby-Smith's surrender of the Trans-Mississippi Department in Texas almost two months later. It was not easy to travel overland to Mexico City. Not only was the terrain rough and arid, the immigrants often had to fight off bandits, guerrilla fighters, and groups of Native Americans who had fled the chaos of the U.S. Civil War. Subsequent immigrants favored traveling by boat to Vera Cruz.[49]

Some of the former Confederates who went to Mexico in the first waves were drawn by what appeared to be an aristocratic society that they believed might be compatible with the values and traditions of "the Southern way of life." Among these die-hard "Chivalrics" were some who had refused the amnesty negotiated at the time of Lee's surrender and saw Mexico as a possible staging ground for launching raids into the United States.[50] Some were politicians ineligible for amnesty and unwilling to risk waiting for what would turn out to be the Andrew Johnson administration's increasingly generous policy of pardons and amnesties. Such fears were reasonable in the political climate of the Union after Confederate sympathizers assassinated President Lincoln shortly after Lee's surrender. That Union troops had arrested and jailed former CSA president Jefferson Davis for treason seemed to confirm those fears.[51]

These new immigrants found that Mexico was also in the throes of a civil war. In 1862 the French emperor Napoleon III (Louis Bonaparte, nephew of Napoleon) sent troops into Mexico on the pretext of collecting unpaid Mexican debts while the United States was preoccupied by sectional conflict. The British and Spanish troops who initially accompanied the French adventure soon withdrew, but the French persisted. After a year they managed to overthrow the Mexican president, Benito Juárez, and set up Austrian archduke Ferdinand Maximilian as the emperor of Mexico in 1864.

Although Mexican conservatives and Catholic clergy supported Maximilian, his regime was always precarious, and he soon faced a formidable guerrilla insurgency led by Juárez.[52] In order to bolster the imperial government with veteran troops and administrators with a congenial social vision, Maximilian and the French had been advocating mass immigration by U.S. Confederates since 1863. To direct this effort, Maximilian appointed Commodore Matthew Fontaine Maury as imperial commissioner of immigration.[53] Although Maury's snobbishness toward nonelite Confederates and disdain for Mexicans made his appointment less than a rousing success, he employed numerous active agents in the U.S. South who were responsible for inaccurate and deceptive advertisements. Maury and his agents hinted that debt peonage might become a form of coercive labor control in Mexico, thus restoring a version of semislavery.

The participants in the Confederate exodus to Mexico had not done the research and preliminary scouting that would have helped them to understand the fluidity of Mexican politics. They were caught by surprise when their welcome suddenly cooled off. The Union victory made both the French and Mexican governments eager to establish good relations with the U.S. government, and the Confederate immigrants suddenly became an embarrassment. Maximilian forbade the Confederates to organize as military units and had them dispersed in rural areas far from the U.S. border.

The largest and most assertive of the Confederate settlements, located about fifty miles west of Vera Cruz near Córdoba, was named Carlota after Mexico's empress. As soon as Maximilian made the grant, Confederate generals and politicians close to Maury claimed 50,000 acres of the best land in order to sell it at inflated prices to immigrants from the U.S. South.[54] The former Confederate elite's effort to maintain old patterns of deference compounded the initial resentment of these immigrants, and many were not used to the extreme physical labor required to create ranchos in the Mexican countryside. Some were less than wholesome types, and disease, hunger, and the hostility of neighbors dispossessed by Maximilian's grant to the Confederates made life extremely difficult.[55] These pressures did not produce a culture of cooperation, harmony, diligence, and respect. As an anonymous U.S. visitor to the colony observed, "American character is associated with whiskey, braggadocio, rudeness, dishonesty, and indolence."[56]

But while the prospects of the colony were not bright in the best of circumstances, its end did not come as a result of internal dissention and hardship. In 1866 Napoleon III began the withdrawal of French troops from Mexico, and events went downhill rapidly for the former Confederates. Supported by U.S. financiers (including Ulysses S. Grant) and demobilized Union soldiers, Benito Juárez's forces toppled the imperial government and executed Maximilian on June 19, 1867. Well before then, Maury and several other prominent Confederates who had convinced settlers to come to Mexico on the strength of their reputations slipped quietly out of Mexico.

The settlers were on their own in a hostile country. Local people reclaiming their lands and Juárez's forces quickly destroyed the settlement.[57] Those who managed to escape by ship from Vera Cruz either returned to the United States or went on to Brazil or British Honduras. A few individual former Confederates did stay on in Mexico, mostly in urban areas, and some became successful journalists, physicians, lawyers, and advisers to the new government but not members of a community of former Confederates.[58]

Swett mentioned in the "Prefatory Remarks" that he had received a letter about emigration to Mexico, but by the time he wrote these remarks Juárez had triumphed, Maximilian had been executed, and Mexicans had destroyed all but one or two colonies of former Confederates.[59] Swett, apparently, was not yet aware that Mexico was no longer a feasible destination for Confederate emigration.[60] The disaster that had befallen the Confederate settlers in Mexico must have sent chills through anyone contemplating expatriation, but agents for the government of Brazil and private entrepreneurial ventures in Brazil, Venezuela, and British Honduras continued to be active and effective in recruiting immigrants.

Brazil drew the largest number of Confederate exiles, and the Confederate expatriates in Brazil are the best researched of the Confederate communities abroad.[61] In the 1860s Brazil was a slave society governed by an emperor, features that many Southerners found appealing.[62] The Brazilian government aggressively courted Confederates as potential supporters of a decaying aristocratic order and the institution of slavery. Large tracts of land could be purchased on favorable terms from the Brazilian government with the condition that the purchasers would recruit people from the U.S. South as settlers. Agents working on commission for these private entrepreneurs, then, were additional sources of self-interested propaganda about the advantages of immigrating to Latin America.[63]

But recruiters, whether working for a foreign government or for a private speculator, were not the only sources of information. Many former Confederates who went to Brazil were members of a network of local colonization societies that hired agents to scout out the potential for immigration—precisely the role in Central America for which Swett volunteered. And since the emigration to Brazil lasted so much longer than emigration to Mexico, information about the route and living conditions there became available through commercial channels. Later arrivals were able to benefit from the letters coming back from ex-Confederates in Brazil, letters sent to friends, families, and local newspapers. These immigrants were therefore better prepared for their life as settlers in a foreign country than their counterparts who went so hastily to Mexico.

Nevertheless, many Southerners who arrived in Brazil were woefully uninformed about the nature of Brazilian race relations. Although it was still a slave society, Brazil did not have the kinds of race politics with which white Southerners were comfortable. More than a few former Confederates were so appalled by the number of very black individuals in positions of respect and authority when they arrived (physicians, naval lieutenants, and Rio de Janeiro's harbor master, for example) that they returned immediately to the United States.[64]

Although Brazil attracted large numbers of ex-Confederates, very few expatriate communities lasted beyond a few years. Most people returned to the United States, but a handful did become successful ranchers or planters, including those few who arrived with enough capital to buy an already operating plantation complete with slaves. The majority of Confederates who remained in Brazil abandoned rural life and moved into towns and cities to establish businesses or professional practices (dentistry was often mentioned). Both sets of these colonists who remained in Brazil became, by necessity, thoroughly assimilated into Brazilian society and culture.

One or two small U.S. settlements in Brazil endured, and these communities did retain more of their U.S. Southern cultural roots. The best known of these is the town of Vila Americana (formerly Santa Bárbara) north of São Paulo, later publicized in articles in popular U.S. magazines complete with photographs of Confederate flags prominently displayed on buildings and monuments. There is a certain irony in the fact that much of the town's viability was due to the commercially successful introduction of a U.S. variety of watermelon.

Although Venezuela drew many fewer Confederates than Mexico, Brazil, and British Honduras, the Venezuela project was notable for its definitive failure and the whiff of fraud.[65] The Venezuelan government was eager to populate eastern regions that were in dispute with the British, whose colony of what was then known as British Guyana had a tendency to expand into contested Venezuelan territory. The Venezuelan government was therefore willing to grant a large tract of land to Dr. Henry Manore Price from the United States to populate the region with people who recognized Venezuela's claims. Although he had never been to Venezuela, Dr. Price enthusiastically recruited Southerners with inducements of mineral wealth and the good life in Venezuela and sold shares in the enterprise to those interested in becoming settlers. Several shiploads of Southern settlers had uniformly unfortunate experiences and high rates of mortality, and one of the U.S. agents, a Mrs. Pattison, recruited seventy British citizens in a financial fraud that almost led to her prosecution after many of them were not only conned but died.

One of the agents for Price's Venezuelan scheme in New Orleans, Mary de Caulp (aka Loreta Janeta Velázquez), was a Cuban who had fought for the Confederacy as Lieutenant Harry T. Buford in Texas and Arkansas cavalry regiments until "he" was discovered to be a she.[66] In her autobiography, Valázquez reported that she had accompanied colonists to Price's land in Venezuela in order to advise friends who were considering emigration, so her motives for traveling seem to have been similar to Charles Swett's. She described her trip in plausible and fascinating detail, but Velázquez's rendition differs from Swett's in two important ways: the veracity of her memoir continues to be debated; and she had an ax to grind with the Venezuelan project. When she published her memoir, a New Orleans newspaper exposed her past, and the Venezuelan recruitment agency fired her. Price had been trying to convince the U.S. government to help him obtain compensation for what he claimed was the Venezuelan government's unfair abrogation of his colonization agreement. She mounted a scathing indictment of Price and his entire organization, which she said was dishonest and dangerous to participants. Modern accounts agree.[67]

Exploring British Honduras

Charles Swett and his party planned to explore only British Honduras, which at that time was another site of significant immigration by former Confederates looking for new homes. Before discussing Swett's experiences there, we need to understand what he saw and what he missed.

A Brief History of British Honduras

British Honduras was a small outpost of British colonialism. The first official census in 1861 reported 25,625 people, making it a small country of citizens even by Central American standards.[68] More than half the population was in the northern provinces, which had received hundreds of refugees from the Yucatán peninsula when eastern Mexico was convulsed by the Caste Wars that began in 1847. The first refugees were Mexicans escaping the indigenous people who rose up against centuries of oppression, and after the revolt was suppressed, indigenous people fled reprisals by the Mexican government. When British Honduras expanded to its current geographical size in the 1850s, its 8,868 square miles put it somewhere between the size of Massachusetts and New Hampshire. The British hung on to the small colony over the centuries against pressures from Spain, Mexico, Guatemala, and hostile indigenous people on the northern border, who conducted raids against British colonists well into the 1880s.[69]

The British Honduran economy had been stagnant for years before the U.S. Civil War. The market for logwood, used to make dyes, was in decline because of competition from chemical dyes. British Honduran mahogany exports began to recede in the 1850s as more mahogany, primarily from Honduras and Nicaragua, was becoming available on the world market. The shift from wooden ships to steel ships reduced the demand for mahogany, and as cutting reduced the number of trees near the coast and major rivers, the remaining desirable trees in British Honduras were located in remote places from which they were difficult and expensive to transport to market.[70]

By the 1850s the economic and political leadership in Belize had concluded that developing a vigorous export agriculture was necessary to supplement the mahogany trade. The largest and most influential landowners in British Honduras were two companies—Young, Toledo, and Company, Ltd. and British Honduras Company, Ltd.—that had received their vast grants of land through connections with the British royal family. They decided

Table 1. Estimated populations and population densities around 1860
(1,000 people, 1,000 square miles)

	1860		
	National Area	Estimated Population	Density (per sq. mi.)
Guatemala	42.0	951	22.6
Honduras	43.3	230	5.3
El Salvador	8.1	424	52.3
Nicaragua	57.1	230	4.0
Costa Rica	19.7	115	5.9
Br. Honduras	8.9	26	0.3

Sources: R. L. Woodward Jr., "Central America from Independence to c. 1870," in *The Cambridge History of Latin America*, vol. 3, *From Independence to c. 1870*, ed. L. Bethell, 478 (New York: Cambridge University Press, 1986); John Alder Burdon, *Archives of British Honduras*, vol. 3, *From 1841 to 1884*, 238 (London: Sifton Praed, 1935).

that the first step toward agricultural development was to bring in pliable agricultural laborers who would work for low wages, always a difficult task in the hot, humid, disease-ridden, and overgrown potential "fields" of British Honduras.

These pliable laborers seemed to be nowhere to be found. Logging, not the cultivation of sugar on large plantations, had been the mainstay of the economy of British Honduras. Slaves had been forced to do heavy labor and agricultural work until emancipation but then had other choices in the city of Belize or around the Caribbean; they could also purchase their own land. So-called Caribs (Garifuna), descendents of runaway slaves and indigenous people from the Honduran and British Honduras coast, had established small trading, fishing, and farming communities around Stann Creek and Punta Gorda in the early nineteenth century, and men from those communities and some migrating workers made up a small proportion of the wage-labor force, mostly in logging.[71] The 1857 Sepoy Mutiny against British colonial authorities in India produced a number of people to be "transported" (that is, deported) from India. The British government allocated 1,000 of the mutineers and their families to British Honduras in 1858.[72] The silence in official records suggests that if they did arrive, most became independent farmers and fishers rather than indentured workers available for employment by the large landowners.

Frederick R. Seymour, the lieutenant governor in 1862 and 1863, agreed with the idea that British Honduras needed more agricultural employees and promoted the immigration of free African Americans from the United States.[73] As early as mid-1851 the governor of Jamaica forwarded a "circular dispatch" to the superintendent of British Honduras suggesting the immigration of some of the "black and coloured population from the United States."[74] During the U.S. Civil War, British officials' willingness to host black colonists from the United States in British Honduras coincided with President Lincoln's interest in colonization schemes and with the financial interest of a U.S. land speculator with contacts in the Lincoln administration.[75]

The proposal to expatriate freed U.S. blacks goes back at least to Thomas Jefferson, but there was a resurgence of interest in the idea among Northern whites in the 1850s and early 1860s, and President Lincoln and several members of his administration were interested in the possibility. But by the end of 1863 the Lincoln administration was backing away from colonization and its most zealous supporters. The disaster resulting from establishing a colony of U.S. former slaves on the Haitian island of L'Ille à Vac, opposition from Central American governments, and resistance by most African Americans, who rejected what they viewed as deportation, all played a role in the decision to drop colonization for the moment.[76]

Meanwhile, the U.S. consul in Belize fought strenuously against the idea of bringing in freed U.S. blacks, arguing that work conditions in British Honduras were so awful that no U.S. citizen should be encouraged to emigrate there, an indication of the effect that the U.S. Emancipation Proclamation was already having on the mindset of some U.S. policy makers. And in December 1863 the British government wrote the governor of Jamaica "forbidding any action to be taken for the introduction of Negroes from the United States in British Honduras."[77]

Lieutenant Governor John Austin arrived in Belize to assume his new post in October 1863. He continued the effort to recruit agricultural workers, and in 1864 the British Honduras Company sponsored the immigration of indentured agricultural workers from China. The experiment was unsuccessful from the point of view of the landowning companies, their local agents, and especially the workers. Of the 454 Chinese workers brought into British Honduras by the company in 1865, death and desertion left only 211 alive and accounted for by 1869. The lieutenant governor concluded that mistreatment, bad food, and overwork were the causes of the Chinese workers' deaths, their desertions, and their September 1865 revolt.[78] The landowning companies then agreed, reluctantly, to Belize merchants' desire to bring in experienced agriculturists from the Confederate states. At least the landowning companies could sell them land, although the merchants criticized the companies for refusing to lower land prices.

Lieutenant Governor Austin promoted the recruitment of former Confederates by subsidizing steamer service between Belize and New Orleans—the *Trade Wind* on which Swett traveled—and guaranteeing new immigrants the service of a surveyor as well as free transportation to sites they considered settling. At $5.00 an acre, however, land in British Honduras was more expensive than in Brazil and Honduras, and after losing a number of prominent potential settlers from the U.S. South because of the price of land, it was clear that something else would have to be done.

With the backing of the Belize merchants, the political leadership of British Honduras softened the $5.00-an-acre price in 1866 by stipulating that a purchaser could work Crown land for five years without paying anything and then pay $1.00 an acre for the next five years. The private companies also lowered their prices on some less desirable logged-over areas. In another initiative, Austin granted a 300,000-acre tract of Crown land (the "Icacos grant") in mid-1867 to former New Orleans cotton broker James M. Putnam on the condition that he recruit fifty families from the U.S. South in two years and 250 more people in five years to colonize the area.[79]

The merchant community in Belize was enthusiastic about these changes, but neither the large landowning companies nor the British imperial bureaucracy shared that enthusiasm. The idea of spending money to make money was antithetical to Britain's colonial principle of empire on the cheap, and the Icacos grant was the last straw. With the support of the private landholding companies, British colonial officialdom recalled Austin in August 1867 and appointed James Robert Longdon to replace him.[80]

Despite the loss of Austen's eager support for immigrants from the U.S. South, prospective immigrants kept arriving. Consular reports estimated that the arrivals from the U.S. South averaged about thirty a week and that in the two years between 1867 and 1869, the rate was around fifty a week. At the same time, the reports emphasized that many would-be immigrants returned home almost immediately and predicted that all this movement would result in slight or no net effect on the size of British Honduras's population.[81]

Charles Swett in British Honduras

Charles Swett and his companions from Warren County traveled to New Orleans the day after Christmas, 1867, and two days later they joined other potential settlers and boarded the steamship *Trade Wind*. After several delays, the ship with its crew and one hundred passengers left New Orleans for British Honduras.

Swett began his diary with some emotional (and stilted) paragraphs about leaving home, but soon moved into a description of the thoroughly unpleasant voyage to British Honduras, at times with a humorous tone. As difficult as Swett found the passage between New Orleans and Belize, his trip was far more comfortable than those of many former Confederates traveling to Belize and elsewhere. Swett and his fellow travelers were on a steamship rather than a sailing ship and therefore less dependent on the vicissitudes of wind. The stories of sailing ships loaded with would-be Confederate expatriates are full of accounts of being blown off course, wrecked on rocky coasts, and becalmed for days at a time.[82]

No matter how the ship was propelled, outbreaks of cholera, typhoid, yellow fever, and smallpox on board often were disasters for crew and passengers alike. Sea travel was very dangerous. Just a few months before Swett and his friends began the journey, the *Trade Wind* had been quarantined in Belize harbor for a deadly outbreak of yellow fever on board, and a year and a half after Swett concluded the trip, the *Trade Wind* sank seventy miles south of the Mississippi River's mouth. Swett's party was more fortunate; seasickness—a common theme among nineteenth-century travel writers— was the principal problem that Swett reported on this trip of the *Trade Wind*.[83]

Swett's description of his fellow travelers in this initial stage of the journey did not identify those whom he mentioned in the first sentence of the "Prefatory Remarks": "Several friends and relatives entertaining the idea of visiting Belize . . . expressed a wish that I should accompany them." Nor did he mention whether the people who had suggested he make the trip were on board the *Trade Wind*, or explain which Daniel Swett was a member of the exploration party listed in the January 6 entry. Daniel Swett might have been Charles's sixty-three-year-old father but was more likely Charles's twenty-two-year-old brother, a surviving veteran of Swett's Battery.

One of the fourteen men on the exploration party list was a colonel, but there were no generals or governors. The men on the list who appear in the multivolume *War of the Rebellion* were lower-level commissioned officers, and their ages were probably close to Charles Swett's thirty-eight years.[84] Charles Swett has many more entries in *War of the Rebellion* than Colonel Harrison, and there is no discernible connection among the men's wartime service. The absence of all these names from such late-nineteenth-century biographical dictionaries as Francis Drake's *Dictionary of American Biography* (1872), *Appleton's Cyclopaedia of American Biography* (1877), and the

National Cyclopedia of American Biography (1898–) suggests that while these men were substantial citizens in their localities, they were not eminent in state or national arenas.[85] But Charles Swett was clearly delighted with his fellow travelers: "We have a most excellent list of passengers." He also notes that these were men "who before the war were in affluent circumstances" (January 2). They were not "poor whites" but from the old elite of the South.

The City of Belize

When Swett landed in Belize, he was surprised at how attractive the city was. After all, his expectations were not high. On the first page of the "Prefatory Remarks," he had described the whole of British Honduras with derision. "We have every reason to believe that country to be covered with jungle and lagoons, from which, the exhalation of phosphuretted and Carburetted hydrogen gas, consequent upon the decomposition of animal and vegetable matter, must be so great as almost to prevent the possibility of strangers escaping its influence."

Not only did the small city have a pleasant prospect, Swett considered Lieutenant Governor James Robert Longdon, the colony's executive officer, to be an outstanding gentleman. Although Great Britain had disappointed Southerners by not coming to the aid of the Confederacy, Swett was predisposed to like British government officials who, in his opinion, operated "the best government on earth" (January 7). Perhaps one factor in its favor was that the British Honduras government conducted its business in the English language. His effusive praise for Longdon is odd, because by his own description, Longdon was clear that he would not go out of his way to extend any help to the potential colonists. Longdon also disappointed many in the party when he told them that they were not eligible for British citizenship. They could count on the support and protection of the British government only when residing in British Honduras and would not be eligible to vote. Swett apparently did not realize that Lieutenant Governor Longdon had recently replaced Lieutenant Governor John Austin, who in the eyes of his superior—the governor of Jamaica—had exceeded his authority in his zeal to attract Confederate colonists to British Honduras.

Looking for Sites in British Honduras

Swett and his party visited some sugar plantations as they sailed down the coast. Although the "Prefatory Remarks" were focused on "the staple" (cotton), his assessment of agricultural prospects in British Honduras revolved around the cultivation of sugar. He had learned from the experiences of earlier Confederate immigrants and the Louisiana planters in his own party that rainfall and insects prevented the cultivation of cotton and that sugarcane was more likely to be successful.

When they were south of the Icacos grant, the exploration party split into smaller groups in order to cover more ground. Swett and his companions went up the Middle and Goldstream rivers, and after their two-day foray met the schooner at the mouth of the Moho River. The next day they ascended the Moho to meet another one of their groups. Swett's descriptions of local practices and landscapes are perceptive, precise, clear, and engaging. Did this involvement suggest that despite his initial serious reservations about emigration and devotion to cotton cultivation, Swett might be willing to immigrate to British Honduras?

The exploratory groups reported their findings, and none of them was very encouraging. Another party of former Confederates engaged in the same endeavor met Swett's group on the Moho and echoed these dreary results. (True to Swett's commitment to his role, he drew no conclusions.) Despite these rather tepid findings, one member of his party was favorably impressed. The Reverend Levi Pearce would return to British Honduras from Honduras and become the leader of Toledo, located between the Moho River and the Rio Grande and the most long-lived of the Confederate communities in British Honduras.

From the Moho River and the Rio Grande, Swett and his companions sailed south to the port of Livingston in Guatemala. Swett was sarcastic about the quarantine that prevented their disembarking and exploring some of the Rio Dulce and Lake Isabel [Izabal]. His attitude is surprising, because he must have known that cholera was a serious threat that could kill hundreds and turn over governments. Moreover, Swett seemed unaware that his party arrived in the city of Belize at the end of a three-week outbreak of cholera that had killed an estimated 150 people.[86] It is possible that Swett's group was deliberately not told about that deadly outbreak of cholera.

Swett's party gave up going ashore, bought some fish and rum, and sailed for Honduras in order to visit the Confederate community near San Pedro Sula. When they arrived in the port of Omoa, they were again threatened with quarantine.

Nineteenth-Century Travelogue Writing

Swett adopted a style in his diary that drew on conventions of travel writing at the time, such as emphasizing the dire hardships and minor annoyances of traveling. But his descriptions also include unusual moments of levity, often in a self-deprecatory tone. For most writers, emphasizing the difficulties of traveling was a way in which an author could present himself or herself away from home as being intrepid, strong, and resourceful. In the words of Mary Louise Pratt: "In many [nineteenth-century travel] accounts, the itinerary itself becomes the occasion for a narrative of success, in which travel is a triumph in its own right. . . . The travelers struggle in unequal battle against scarcity, inefficiency, laziness, discomfort, poor horses, bad roads, bad weather, delays."[87]

From Swett's account, we would add insects, seasickness, sleeping on a boat's cabin roof in rainstorms, and walking miles through difficult terrain. While occasionally referring to similar trials as a Civil War soldier, his self-deprecation suggests that boasting was not his intention. He admits that he "was one of the first to succumb [to seasickness], notwithstanding the remedy [whiskey] above spoken of, and the most powerful exercise of the will in connection" (December 30). On January 8 there was an invasion of sand flies, and on January 9 there was the hiring of a second schooner formerly occupied by swine, and travel delays that required them to "exercise patience, our stocks of which we did not find excessive, as requisition has to be made in that direction very frequently, for very large quantities, to be delivered in the very best order, and immediately." These details contribute to his credibility as a dispassionate recorder of events relying solely on "occular demonstration," although in many ways he is writing an anti-travelogue.

Swett was not seeking, as did many nineteenth-century travel writers, to produce a best-selling book that would earn him significant royalties. Like those traveling to Brazil on the behalf of potential emigrants, he was more of a scout, weighing the feasibility of success for disaffected Southerners in new places. He was not a romantic reveling in the beauty of nature, a scientist excited about the discovery of new plants and animals, or an investor seeking to profit from incorporating an "undeveloped" area into the modern market economy, although he commented on many of these themes. He was at his best using his experience in the army and hardware business to describe in clear detail agriculture, tools, and modes of transportation, all of which would provide basic, useful information for future migrants.

Reflecting his sense of purpose, Swett hardly mentioned local people. Thus he was outside the genre of nineteenth-century travel writers who focused on exotic local populations, with particular attention to scantily clad women, in order to titillate their readers and confirm their readers' sense of superiority. His avoidance of dwelling on the exotic was well illustrated in his first real multicultural experience, which occurred in the Carib village at North Stann River (January 11). Instead of giving us a picture of the inhabitants, he described the village houses and the making of cassava bread in terms worthy of the *National Geographic*. Not only do no scantily clad women appear in the Carib village, there are, for all intents and purposes, no women anywhere in the entire pamphlet, perhaps another way of casting Central America as "not" a potential home.[88]

The Place of Race

Although English speaking, around 90 percent of the local people in Belize and British Honduras were of African descent. So how did Swett deal with this? One clue is that when he lists the names of men from the *Trade Wind* who would form the party of exploration, he ends with "and last, though not an unimportant personage, Wm. Owens, an 'American citizen of African descent'" (January 6). The use of "citizen," although included within Swett's quotation marks, is surprising, and the entire phrase is civil, albeit perhaps a bit snide.

But beyond describing a colleague's servant, Swett's description of the church congregation in Belize (insert within January 6 entry) is very different from the attitude of his "Prefatory Remarks" on the subject of race: "We attended service here at night, two hundred or more of the colored population being present, and only *three white persons*, that we could see, and we never saw a more quiet or attentive congregation. The moment we appeared at the door, we were politely conducted to a seat, and every attention shown that could anywhere be given."

Not only is the harangue on race relations in Swett's "Prefatory Remarks" absent in his diaries, Swett's treatment of blacks is measured, even respectful. He intended to publish the essay that appears in the pamphlet as "Prefatory Remarks" by itself, thus addressing a more general readership than the diaries, which were targeted at prospective emigrants. But more important than its intended audience, Swett's rant in the "Prefatory Remarks" was inspired by what he saw as efforts to overturn the "natural social order" of white supremacy rather than against people of color per se, with whom he had extensive experience under the old racial order. While there appeared to be more racial equality in British Honduras than there would be in the U.S. South for more than a century, Swett did not seem to be threatened by the presence of the black majority.

Charles Swett's apparent tolerance of blacks in British Honduras was different from that of a large number of Confederate immigrants. By 1868 Southern exiles in British Honduras had already earned an unsavory reputation for drunkenness and violence, especially against blacks, and the locals—black and white—were beginning to regret encouraging them to come. This was evident in an article in the *British Honduras Colonist and Belize Advertiser* (October 24, 1868) just a few months after Swett's party first visited Belize. The article was about yet another assault by an armed Southerner on a black British Honduran. The newspaper forcefully asserted that "our laws will not permit [it], public feeling will not endure it; and if the persons who immigrate to our shore in search of homes . . . cannot keep their violent and lawless passions under control, it would be far better that they remained under the tender and merciful care of Major-General Butler."[89]

Why would people allergic to dealing with free blacks consider immigrating to a place like British Honduras, where people of African descent made up the overwhelming majority? Property restrictions on the franchise diluted blacks' political influence in British Honduras, which certainly was no paradise of racial equality. But British Honduras was not characterized by the racial hostilities of the U.S. South or British West Indies.

A glimpse of this can be seen in the views of Dr. Stephen Lushington, a member of the British Parliament and an opponent of racial divides in the British West Indies. He issued a report on "the condition of the free people of Colour at Honduras" to the British colonial secretary dated October 28, 1827. In the report, Lushington was critical of the high property requirements for colored men to vote or serve in the legislative assembly, and he points out some other discriminatory practices. But he also notes that there were twelve men of color in the assembly, along with twenty-eight white men. In addition, "Nearly two thirds of the whole property at Honduras in Land, Slaves, and personality belong to the free coloured class exclusive of the free blacks. . . . And there is also this remarkable difference that at the Honduras all classes of white and brown mix in society, whereas in Jamaica the brown race are wholly excluded. The prejudice on account of Colour is at the Honduras comparatively very small."[90]

No one would argue that British Honduras was heaven on earth for people of African descent, but the colony had been making steady progress toward more racial equality. Free blacks in British Honduras had been given important new rights in 1831, when the British Honduras government passed "An Act to Entitle all His Majesty's Coloured Subjects of Free Condition in this Settlement and their issue to the same Rights and privileges with British Subjects of White Parents."[91] The British government abolished slavery in the British Empire through a gradual, compensated process that lasted from 1834 to 1838. And white families routinely went to church with black families. White Southerners could have avoided such voluntary sociability, but there was a deeper problem for them: there were a number of black people in positions of authority, people the Southerners had to deal with on an equal footing. As a consequence, there was a steady recurrence of nasty incidents between former Confederates and black policemen, customs officers, and other lower-level officials.[92]

How could former Confederates manage to live in British Honduras with its predominantly black population and positions of trust and respect occupied by people of color? The solution was to stake out acreage in isolated areas and create enclaves hermetically sealed from the host society. Toledo, the largest and most durable Confederate community in British Honduras, was the most successful in this regard. The Reverend Levi Pearce, whom Swett had described as being determined to emigrate although he had never seen the country (December 29), founded Toledo with his family upon leaving Swett's party in the Republic of Honduras.

Toledo did manage to cut itself off from the broader society and to protect itself from the need to deal with people of African descent as equals, much less as authorities. But Pearce's community adhered to such a strict form of Methodism that it cut itself off from even other Confederate exiles. From sixty-six residents in early 1868, the membership in the community declined rapidly. Nevertheless, a handful of families in Toledo managed to hold on for almost forty years.[93]

But the other communities of former Confederates collapsed. In 1868 the British Honduras lieutenant governor reported that there were fewer than 500 immigrants from the U.S. South still in the colony, and official censuses, taken first in 1861 and thereafter every ten years, never found more than 125 residents in British Honduras who were born in the United States.[94]

Nothing that Charles Swett saw in British Honduras was attractive enough to change his mind about emigrating, but he was about to embark upon a side trip to the Republic of [Spanish] Honduras and the community of former Confederates near San Pedro Sula in order to "verify or disprove by occular demonstration the extravagant stories we have heard of the Republic" (January 10).

DEAD END IN HONDURAS

Swett and his colleagues had not planned to visit Honduras, but if they had, they could have obtained considerable information about the region in English before leaving the United States. While communications in the

U.S. South in the years immediately following the Civil War were disrupted, it would not have been difficult to obtain one of the widely circulating travel books about Spanish-speaking Central America. This literature stood in sharp contrast to the paucity of published information about British Honduras.[95]

While official U.S. government presence in Central America during the 1840s and 1850s had been minimal, there was a market in the mid-nineteenth-century U.S. reading public for Central American themes.[96] The first draw was the importance of creating a trans-isthmus railroad or canal in order to reduce the length and danger of the trip from the U.S. Atlantic coast to the U.S. Pacific coast after the Mexican War (1846–1848), when the United States became a continent-wide nation and the California gold rush soon followed. Many wanted to go to California, and if that was not feasible, they delighted in reading about the adventures of those who did. The printed literature had been echoed in diaries kept by migrants to California and their letters back home. In 1851 Cornelius Vanderbilt, the steamship magnate, established the lucrative Accessory Transit Company serving travelers between the two coasts. A steamship took passengers from New York to San Juan del Norte, on the Nicaraguan–Costa Rican border. At that point passengers transferred to small steamships that went up the San Juan River into Lake Nicaragua. From there it was a coach ride of only fifteen or twenty miles to the Pacific coast, where they boarded another steamer for California.

Thousands went to California via Vanderbilt's route, preferring it to sailing around Cape Horn or going overland from St. Louis. His route was also superior to a similar, competitive line that went by steamboat to Panama, by mule-back to the Pacific coast, and by steamship to California. Vanderbilt's route was safer and 500 miles and a couple of days shorter than the Panama alternative, although this changed when U.S. investors opened a rail line across Panama in 1855. In the 1850s Ephraim G. Squier, a renowned anthropologist and author, proposed building a railroad across Honduras, and he received some incentives from the Honduran government. Nevertheless, he was unable to procure adequate financing in the United States and Europe, and the Honduran Inter-Oceanic Railroad (HIOR) was never completed.[97]

U.S. interest in Central America in the 1850s was also heightened by speculators' promotion of the mineral and other natural resources that allegedly could enrich enterprising business interests from the United States. These promotions went beyond investment opportunities by trying to stimulate migration to Honduras by U.S. whites. Both Ephraim Squier and William

V. Wells, through pamphlets, brochures, and their travel books, advertised what appeared to offer North Americans entirely new and prosperous lives in ways similar to the marketing of foreign sites for former Confederates after the Civil War. To complement his railroad project, Squier touted the potential rewards of agriculture and ranching, and Wells emphasized the promise of mining in Honduras. Both published books that attracted large U.S. readerships.

A third source of interest in Central America by the U.S. public was the temporary success of William Walker and his small U.S.-recruited army in taking over the Nicaraguan government from 1855 to 1857. A coordinated assault by the other four Central American nations' armies defeated Walker and his group of U.S. adventurers ("filibusters"). When Walker returned to Central America and invaded Trujillo, Honduras, in 1860, the Honduran army responded in force, and Walker surrendered to the British to avoid capture by Hondurans. The British commander promptly turned him over to Honduran authorities, who executed him. Walker and his escapades were extremely popular in the United States, and especially among Southerners, who avidly followed Walker's rise and fall in the newspapers and weekly magazines.[98] Colonel Henry L. Kinney tried to take over a large portion of eastern Nicaragua and Honduras in the 1850s, and while his adventures were also popular in the United States, Kinney had only meager success in Central America. Interestingly enough, Swett seems to regard the entire Walker and Kinney phenomenon to be irrelevant, despite Walker's attempt to reintroduce slavery in Nicaragua.

Honduras Background

British Honduras possessed neither the economic potential nor the imperialist drama of Spanish Central America, and it must have been difficult for prospective immigrants such as Swett's party to see much that would help with their particular situation. Honduras was somewhat more densely populated than British Honduras, but had experienced decades of depopulation by the 1860s. By the mid-nineteenth century the population had slowly begun to recover, but cholera epidemics and civil wars continued to retard growth.[99] These demographic changes square with Swett's observation that some of the empty land he was seeing had once been cultivated but was now abandoned (January 25, 26, and February 24).

In the first twenty-five years that Honduras was an independent nation (1838–1863), ten governments struggled to bring stability to the country. Ruling party turnovers and civil wars were not caused exclusively by conflicts among local factions; much of the violence and political instability in Honduras had spilled over from region-wide struggles. Although there was no Central American war of independence, there had been recurring violence throughout Central America ever since it broke away from Spain in 1821. After a brief period in which the five states of Central America were a part of the Mexican empire, regional elites unified sufficiently to declare their complete independence as the United Provinces of Central America.[100]

Similar to almost all newly independent Spanish-speaking nations of Latin America, the principal political struggles in Central America were among the white elites and were expressed in the European terms of "Conservatives" versus "Liberals." Conservatives envisioned a strong central government buttressed by an established church and a corporate form of social order characterized more by caste than by class. The European and Spanish American Liberal ideal of political organization was comparatively modern, stressing individualism and capitalism. Liberals rejected the Spanish heritage of Catholicism and aristocracy and aspired to emulate the northern states of the United States.[101]

These differences were not abstractions; they were concrete but divergent strategies to manage and control highly unequal societies. The stakes were especially high in Guatemala, which contained half of the region's population, including a large, unassimilated, and restive Indian majority to a greater extent than elsewhere in Central America.[102] The civil wars generated their own self-feeding momentum. As exile, confiscation, and killing became common elements of the competitive repertoire, revenge and personal animosities contributed to sustaining the violence.

Guatemalan Liberals emerged victorious from a vicious civil war between 1826 and 1829, and they implemented anticlerical reforms and an ambitious liberal economic and social program in Guatemala. The speed and nature of the changes created serious tensions in the countryside, and when Liberal-sponsored northern European immigrants were the source of a devastating cholera epidemic, peasant revolts spread throughout Guatemala.

José Rafael Carrera, an illiterate mestizo swineherd, emerged as the leader of the Indian and mixed-race uprising, and local elites of European descent closed ranks against the common enemy. Nevertheless, Carrera and his informal army swept the field in 1837–1839. It seemed as though the most terrifying nightmare of the privileged Guatemalans had come about, and they were witnessing a true social revolution by the unwashed and nonwhite rural poor. But it was not so; Carrera's movement was trenchantly conservative, eager to abolish the liberal reforms, restore the Church, and revive many colonial institutions and practices, including the corporate Indian communities. Nevertheless, it took a while for Guatemalan Conservatives to recognize how conservative were Carrera and his movement, to overcome their personal distaste for having to deal with him and his like, and finally to ally with him.

Carrera became the most powerful political figure in Central America, and with the exception of one year in the late 1840s, remained so until his death in 1865. In line with Conservative wishes, the United Provinces dissolved in 1838, and the five new nations created their own constitutions. These independent nations were still capable of coordination during emergencies, as in 1857 when they defeated William Walker and his filibusters.

Political and military coordination among the new nations was made easier by Carrera's success in ensuring that friendly Conservatives governed in neighboring countries if not throughout Central America. In Honduras, this required direct military intervention. Since Honduras lacked both an aristocratic elite and large Indian communities, conservatism had no social base. Moreover, the British, allied with Guatemalan Conservatives, occupied the Bay Islands—Honduran islands off the north coast—and encouraged unauthorized logging on Honduras's northern coast. This did not increase the popularity of conservatism in Honduras, especially since Conservatives were not very strong in domestic politics. As a result, the Guatemalan army intervened in the mid-1850s to replace Trinidad Cabañas, a Liberal president, with José Santos Guardiola. When President Guardiola was assassinated in 1862, it took Guatemalan troops almost a year to enable José María Medina, another Conservative, to become president.

Medina was the president when a group of former Confederates established a colony outside San Pedro Sula, and the U.S. settlers named their community for Medina. Honduras's difficult terrain and undeveloped infrastructure made communication slow and unreliable, but Medina, from the capital in Comayagua, succeeded in making his presence felt (and feared) as far away as the northern coast.[103] He had 800 people executed in the province of Olancha after a failed revolt in 1864–1865.

Nevertheless, it turned out that President Medina had policy aspirations inconsistent with Carrera's brand of conservatism. Carrera died in 1865, and his handpicked successor in Guatemala proved to be ineffectual. This freed President Medina to create a program of economic development. He sponsored legislation to stimulate the production and export of coffee, tobacco, and indigo and issued a proclamation in 1866 that outlined a series of rights and privileges for immigrants tailored to make Honduras attractive to expatriates from the U.S. South. Documents 1, 2, and 5 in Appendix A are copies of official government documents from 1866 and 1867 listing generous incentives for immigrants—a classic liberal move contrary to Carrera's and Guardiola's conservative legacy.

Another example of President Medina's breaking free of the Carrera heritage was his granting of a contract to a British firm in 1866 to build a railway from Puerto Caballos/Cortez on the Caribbean coast to the Bay of Fonseca on the Pacific side, a project deeply identified with Honduran Liberal leaders. Ephraim George Squier had convinced Liberal President Cabañas of its value and feasibility, and when the Guatemalans forced Cabañas out of office and brought in Conservative Guardiola, the railroad project languished. With President Medina's support, the railroad reached San Pedro Sula from Puerto Cortéz in 1870, approximately forty miles, but it did not go much farther. It was a great stimulus to the local economy, but the skills and resources necessary for its maintenance were too great for the municipalities, and the railroad shut down in the mid-1870s.[104]

Charles Swett and Green Malcolm in Medina, Honduras

By the time he reached Honduras, Swett was tired and cross. He was particularly testy about the possibility of being delayed by quarantines in Livingston and Omoa, the difficulty of traveling in Honduras, and how casual "those people" were about time (a common North American complaint about Spanish-speaking societies). Unlike his tone in the British Honduras diaries, he no longer conveyed the impression of enjoying his adventure. He implied that Honduras was not a suitable site for emigration and was eager to go home. The travels around Honduras were indeed tedious, and he drove home the lack of adequate transportation. Turning an interesting phrase or being humorous no longer seemed worth the effort to him. He was also ill—on February 10 and 11 with chills, and on March 9 and 10 with seasickness. These are the only days in the entire diary without entries.

When Charles Swett landed in Omoa, he and Colonel Harrison set off east along the coast for "Port Cables."[105] Swett was impressed with the harbor, and he met another group of former Confederates, including Colonel McDermott, looking around the area for a place to settle.[106] When they got back to Omoa (January 20), four members of the group rented a boat and left for various destinations, including Rev. Levi Pearce, who returned to British Honduras to found the settlement of Toledo.

On the way from Omoa to San Pedro Sula on mule-back, Swett and his party stopped at Rancho Grande and made the acquaintance of José

Reynaud, whom Swett mistakenly identified as a governor. The next afternoon they arrived in San Pedro Sula, next to the former Confederates' community of Medina.[107]

Rodolfo Pastor Fasquelle, the principal historian of San Pedro Sula, describes San Pedro Sula in the 1860s as a poor, isolated village with around 600 people. He says that there were no rich people, only some who were not as poor, and that illiteracy was rife (see Document 3 in Appendix A for the number of municipal officials who could not write their names). Pastor Fasquelle describes the arrival of Green Malcolm, former major in the Confederate army, and thirty U.S. families in April 1867 as a complete surprise to the locals: "as though dropped from the sky."[108]

While residents were surprised by the arrival of the former Confederates, what surprised Pastor Fasquelle was the warmth of the reception accorded the newcomers, since San Pedro Sula residents had usually greeted foreigners with suspicion and dislike. There had been some veterans from Walker's failed effort in Nicaragua who had come through San Pedro Sula in the 1850s, and they were such an unsavory lot that the village moved them right along.[109] One would think that the entire filibustering enterprise, including Colonel Henry L. Kinney's and Walker's activities, both of which involved violations of Honduran territory, would have made locals especially wary of U.S. Southerners sympathetic to slavery.

Nevertheless, Appendix A, entitled "Documents Concerning the Settlement of Medina, Honduras," contains a set of official documents that include the 1866 proclamation from the national government (Document 1) outlining the incentives tailored to make Honduras attractive to expatriates from the U.S. South. And Document 3 lists the village's own generous grants to Green Malcolm and his party, dated only twelve days after they arrived in Omoa. The Honduran government promptly responded to Malcolm's initial petition, dated May 3, 1867, and granted Malcolm almost everything that he asked for, although some privileges were qualified or reduced in space or time. The national government augmented the grant of municipal land with a grant of national land, and it ceded to the former Confederates exclusive rights to import certain machines and to manufacture cloth, shingles, tin ware, and so on.

Since the thirty U.S. families in the Medina community no doubt included a number of pious Protestants, it is curious that Malcolm's petition did not mention freedom of religion. On the other hand, both President Medina's 1866 proclamation offering welcome to former U.S. Confederates as well as the government's response to Malcolm's petition assured religious freedom for non-Catholics as long as they worshipped in private.

This gesture may sound overly cautious on the part of President Medina, and although it was consistent with the Honduran constitution, it was still risky. In the late 1850s, when Great Britain relinquished its shaky claim to the Bay Islands, President Guardiola agreed, at Britain's urging, to allow freedom of worship for the British settlers who remained on the Bay Islands. This infuriated the Honduran Catholic clergy, who claimed that the provision violated the Honduran constitution. A number of clerics led a revolt against the government, an event called the "La Guerra de los Padres." The Honduran army crushed the insurrection, but President Medina had to have this in mind when he granted limited freedom of worship to the former Confederates on the mainland.

Charles Swett was quite taken with the San Pedro Sula area. "The town is certainly most delightfully situated, two and a half miles from the mountains on the west, whose tops are frequently enveloped in clouds, and the varying hues of the vegetation on their slopes as the sun rises and descends make a scene that is constantly changing, and which is as pleasing as it is lovely" (inserted between January 22 and 23). He had been surprised and pleased that British Honduras was not as awful as he thought it would be, but still he did not admire its beauty. Nevertheless, getting around in Honduras was simply too difficult, and it was extremely slow and costly to move produce to the port for export. Although Swett was aware of plans for the HIOR, he appeared skeptical about completing a rail connection even to San Pedro Sula.

The Medina settlement was less than nine months old when Swett arrived, and he was not impressed by what had been accomplished in that time. Moreover, Swett did not much like Major Green Malcolm. Swett heaped effusive praise on every transplanted European and U.S. citizen whom he met on the trip, responses that made his silence about the character of Malcolm rather telling. This is odd because, after all, Malcolm had "fought a good war," served in the same Army of Kentucky as Swett, and was only seven years older than Swett. Perhaps Swett's coolness toward the man was due to what we have noted about Swett's generally depressed outlook during his visit to Honduras, but it is also possible he simply disapproved of Malcolm's heavy-handed style.

There is no question that Malcolm was an unusual person. Green Malcolm (1821–1906) was born Abednego Greenberry Malcolm in Kentucky.[110] In 1846 he enlisted to fight in the Mexican War and was a veteran not only of battles in Texas but also the capture of Mexico City. After leaving the army, he resided in both California and Texas before enlisting as a major and second in command of the 1st (McNairy's) Tennessee Cavalry

Battalion, organized early in 1861 and subsequently attached to the Army of Kentucky.[111] Somewhere along the way he acquired some medical skills and presented himself as a physician.

What is not clear, however, is why he left the colony with his wife and two sons in 1870, the very year that a railroad connected San Pedro Sula to the northern coast. Margaret Malcolm Haas, a descendent of Malcolm, says she understood the reasons to be that all four of them became ill in Medina, none of the familiar crops was successful, and the Honduran government reneged on some of its commitments.

The fact that his wife died shortly after reaching the United States supports the first reason. Swett's description of Malcolm's cotton fields threatened by armyworms (January 23 and 29) is consistent with the second. On the third point, the letter from Green Malcolm labeled Document 7 in Appendix A suggests that San Pedro Sula authorities' understanding of their agreement was different from Malcolm's. In addition to these explanations, Elwood Coleman, a descendant of the Medina community's founders, reports that Malcolm was reputed to have "a rather hot temper," which might have hindered the development of a coherent and harmonious community. In any case, Malcolm lived the rest of his eighty-five years in eastern Texas, where he married again, worked as a physician, and had five more children.

Although the Honduran government had offered generous inducements to the Confederate immigrants, the community did not last beyond the early 1870s. By 1875 the U.S consul in Omoa, Trujillo, and Ruatan wrote about the former Confederate immigrants in Medina to the U.S. Department of State as a part of a general survey of Honduras, and he made it sound as though the community had been dissolved years earlier. He stated that the ex-Confederates "engaged in cotton planting, but an insect to them unknown destroyed the Cotton when nearly ready for picking and left them penniless. Their situation was represented as distressing. The great majority of them finaly [sic] worked and begged their way back to their homes, the few that remained engaged in other business, and are doing very well."[112]

After the Medina Community

The Coleman family was one of the most important of those former Confederates who remained in Honduras and were "doing very well."[113] William Allen Coleman (1838–1917), of Carroll County, Georgia, and his brother, John Henry Coleman (1840–1932), both veterans of the 1st Georgia Cavalry, joined Green Malcolm's party to go to Honduras after the war. William Allen's wife, Cynthia Riggs Coleman (1837–1877); two young sons, John W.

(1859–1896) and William Forrest (1864–1944); and William Allen Coleman's sister and her husband, another veteran, left from New Orleans on the *Trade Wind* in 1867. The ship foundered off the coast of Omoa, and while no one died, the Coleman family spent their first night in Omoa cold, wet, hungry, and huddled under a tree.

Although William Allen's brother, sister, and sister's husband soon returned to Georgia, William Allen and his family stayed. Unlike most of the members of the Medina community, William Allen saw some substantial business potential in and around San Pedro Sula, and in 1868 he returned to Georgia to obtain the machinery and tools that he needed for farming and lumbering.

The Coleman family certainly did not fit the stereotype held by some in San Pedro Sula of the immigrants from the U.S. South. Pastor Fasquelle quotes an unnamed local nineteenth-century historian who maintained that the former Confederates had been told that they would be able to establish plantations with unfree workforces (slavery, debt peonage, indenture, and so on) in Honduras, and when they saw that they had been deceived, most of them returned to the United States. Pastor Fasquelle offers no evidence for the claim that the immigrants expected the availability of coerced labor, a claim certainly not suggested in the documents reproduced in Appendix A. Nevertheless, Pastor Fasquelle seems to accept the assertion, although he does note that "several of the deceived slavers stayed to work, first with their hands, and later with migrant labor that began to flow towards the coast [from the interior of the country]."[114] He probably had the Coleman family in mind, a family that thrived in the San Pedro community, intermarried with Hondurans, and became valued citizens.

William Allen Coleman built successful businesses in saw milling, sugarcane, and bananas, and he was able to do all of this without selling his farm in Carroll County. Over time, he became a wealthy man, and he often traveled to the United States in order to take money to his parents. In 1884 William Allen left the Honduras businesses in the hands of his son, William Forrest, and he and his family returned to live in Georgia, where he died in 1917.

There is not much information about John William Coleman, William Allen's oldest son, other than that he served as U.S. consul in San Pedro Sula from 1886 to 1891 and that he died in 1896 in San Pedro Sula. The younger son, William Forrest, left more of a record. He attended Mercer University in Georgia, married Yndelacia Paredes of a wealthy Honduran family in 1880, and had six children. William Forrest successfully ran the Honduran businesses, including two industrial concerns, and Pastor

4. William Allen Coleman (1838–1917) [#5A]. Elwood R. Coleman's Web site, http://www.coleman young.blogspot.com/, accessed July 14, 2010. Reproduced with Elwood R. Coleman's permission.

Fasquelle recognizes the firm of Coleman and Barnes as important in local philanthropy in the 1890s, especially through contributions toward education and road repair.[115]

Pastor Fasquelle observes that foreigners in San Pedro Sula were not discriminated against, but neither did they have any special privileges.[116] William Forrest had an experience in 1916 that illustrates this quite graphically. He refused to pay a one-peso fine (approximately $0.35 US) on the grounds that some (unspecified) house decorations encouraged by the municipality were voluntary, not obligatory. Moreover, his house was outside the city limits, and none of his neighbors with undecorated houses had been fined. Local officials put this fifty-two-year-old personage into a windowless, filthy

5. Cynthia Riggs Coleman (1837–1877) with her son, William Forrest Coleman (1864–1944) [#5]. Elwood R. Coleman's Web site, http://www.coleman-young.blogspot.com/, accessed July 14, 2010. Reproduced with Elwood R. Coleman's permission.

cell without food, water, or a chair to sit on for over five hours. He must have been one of the most important employers in San Pedro Sula, but he was not exempt from arbitrary and severe treatment by local officials.

William Forrest wrote all this to the U.S. consul in San Pedro Sula, and we do not know how or if it was resolved. William Forrest himself was the U.S. consul in San Pedro Sula from 1927 until the post was closed in 1930. He died in San Pedro Sula in 1944.

Pastor Fasquelle estimates that toward the end of the nineteenth century, there were roughly equal numbers of people from England, France, Germany, and the United States in San Pedro Sula. Beyond his mention of their philanthropy, he makes no references to individual U.S. immigrants, but he often notes the activities of European individuals in civic affairs. He does say that the English-speaking immigrants brought an Australian woman to San Pedro in 1880 to teach their children, and in the same year the same immigrant community became so "scandalized" by public nudity among men and women washing clothes and bathing in the river that the municipality built a laundry and bathhouse, segregated by sex.[117]

Returning Home

Given the tone of the Honduras diaries, it is surprising that Charles Swett seriously considered going with James Putnam to look at more real estate when Swett returned to British Honduras on his way back to the United States. Swett apparently had no idea that Putnam himself was becoming tired of the whole exile endeavor. Putnam returned to New Orleans in time for the 1870 census. He was still there in 1880 and died in 1887. T. C. Brewer was the other former Confederate in Belize whom Swett admired, and Brewer and his wife, Ana, closed their hotel and returned to Alabama in 1869, shortly after Swett recommended their hostelry with such warmth. William C. Cary, who established the first regular New Orleans–Belize steamboat service, and W. J. S. Scobell, founder and editor of the newspaper the *Commercial Advertiser*, were other leading members of the Confederate community in Belize who returned to the United States soon after Charles Swett's last visit.[118]

The trip to New Orleans on board the *Trade Wind* was uneventful, but Swett's description of seasickness contained more spirit than his uninspired descriptions of the visit to Honduras. He was obviously pleased to be returning to the United States.

Part II

The Diaries

✳

CHARLES SWETT, *A TRIP TO BRITISH HONDURAS AND TO SAN PEDRO, REPUBLIC OF HONDURAS*

We have mostly preserved the diaries as written by Charles Swett, including the unexplained use of asterisks in the "Prefatory Remarks" and the multiple spelling of the name of the steamship Trade Wind. *We have, however, made a few changes that we considered appropriate for modern readers, including breaking up a couple of the lengthiest paragraphs and inserting a few subtitles. Charles Swett's own subtitles are generally in all capitals and thus easily distinguished from ours. We also rearranged some of the items, placing portions from the appendixes into the daily entries in order to expand the descriptive richness of Charles Swett's observations. Finally, we inserted some material in brackets and footnotes for clarity; the words in parentheses are entirely Charles Swett's.*

PREFACE.

As we have stated in "Prefatory Remarks" that we were opposed to emigration to Honduras, it may be necessary for us to say that we have, in the following account, given a description of what we saw, faithfully, and as far as possible without prejudice.

It was our intention to publish "Prefatory Remarks" at the time the article was written, (October 7, 1867,) but we reserved it for publication in connection with what we should see in Honduras, which is done without altering a word, or the erasure of a single line.

Warren Co., Miss.
April, 1868. CHARLES SWETT

Prefatory Remarks

Several friends and relatives entertaining the idea of visiting Belize, (British Honduras), communicated their intentions to me and expressed a wish that I should accompany them, which I could not consent to do; but promised to think of the matter and to give them an answer before the departure, feeling satisfied they had not fully determined to go; but being assured that they would go I at last consented to accompany them provided nothing should occur to prevent. If they go, it is for the purpose of endeavoring to convince themselves that it is a better country than this, and for the purpose of establishing themselves there if they find the country such as they believe it to be. If I go, it will be for the purpose of gratifying those who desire my company, and with no fixed determination to make it my home, but on the contrary, with every feeling of opposition to that portion of the earth's surface.

We at present know but little of Belize, and even I may find sufficient inducement to go to that country; but at present, if asked whether I think it would be better to make the change, would answer with a decided negative. We have every reason to believe that country to be covered with jungle and lagoons, from which, the exhalation of phosphuretted and Carburetted hydrogen gas, consequent upon the decomposition of animal and vegetable matter, must be so great as almost to prevent the possibility of strangers escaping its influence, and suffering from a malaria that will produce remittent, intermittent and pernicious fevers. This it is reasonable to expect; and how many of those who must necessarily undergo this acclimation will ever enjoy in future the health which was theirs in our own country?

The latitude is further south and nearer the equator, and it is a well authenticated fact that it is more desirable in a Hygienic point of view to remove from a warm to a cold climate, in a majority of instances, than from a northern to a latitude nearer the equator.

Here most of us are acclimated, and if taken sick we have physicians who are acquainted with the diseases of our section, and our peculiar idiosyncrasies, and consequently there would be a better chance of our recovery than would be the case in another latitude, however skillful the treatment of our case might be, if unaccompanied by the circumstances above named. Here we have friends who will rejoice with us in our prosperity, and who will sympathize with us in our misfortunes, which we can not expect in a strange land. In a word, this is home; a land that is ours; doubly ours; having been bequeathed to us by our forefathers, who sacrificed their lives in that war of the revolution, and by those who so recently died in the vain attempt to place our section in a position of independence. Should this country not be dearer than ever to us because of these reflections? Should we not remain here and keep forever green the graves of departed heroes, or should we desert a land that has been bought at such a price, and forget the suffering and privation of those who are now beyond reach of our sympathy, and whom no word of encouragement can reach, but whose memories we should cherish, and whose deeds we should keep forever fresh in our memories? Should we forget the midnight bivouac and scanty meal, with the cold wet ground for our bed and the canopy of heaven our only covering? The long and tiresome marches, through rain, snow, and ice, with naked feet and ragged clothing? Should we banish the recollection of all this from our minds, and leave blank the place now occupied by such hallowed memories?

No, let us deliberate well before we leave our homes. It is a serious matter at any time, and particularly so at the present. It is a step that should not be taken without the most careful and exhaustive consideration, and until we are satisfied the change will be greatly to our advantage. Immediately after the close of the war, a distinguished confederate general, in a letter to myself, stated it to be his determination to go to Mexico should it be necessary for him to leave here, yet at the same time stated it to be his determination to remain here as long as he could, and said he would advise all to do so as long as it could be done with honor and safety.[1]

At the time of receiving the letter I contemplated going to Mexico, but the whole current of my thoughts was changed, and I almost came to the positive conclusion to remain here as long as it could be done with "honor and safety." Since then, events have rapidly transpired which have been of a character to almost justify a determination to change, yet such was not my feeling at the time the contemplated trip was made known to me, nor is it at present; though, under a certain condition of things, any land might possibly be better than our own, which condition has not yet arrived, and I

---

1. The "distinguished confederate general" might have been General Thomas C. Hindman, who was Swett's commander in the early days of the war (Swett 1908: 5). Hindman became the head of the Trans-Mississippi army before Kirby-Smith, and he did indeed go to Mexico. Diane Neal and Thomas W. Kremm, *Lion of the South: General Thomas C. Hindman* (Macon, Ga.: Mercer University Press, 1993); Andrew F. Rolle, *The Lost Cause: The Confederate Exodus to Mexico* (Norman: University of Oklahoma Press, 1965), 116.

sincerely hope it may never be our misfortune to witness. Since the late war, thousands have left this country with the view of bettering their condition, and many more contemplate leaving, notwithstanding the fact that few, if any, of all who made the change have been able to render such an account of their new homes as to induce their friends to follow. Many have gone, and more will go without giving the subject the consideration it demands, but make the leap in the dark, and without calculating the result if they fail to leap the chasm, and should reach the bottom of an unfathomable abyss of future misery, want and suffering.

We have from time to time been visited by so called agents of foreign and more favored lands (?) who, in too many instances care very little what ultimately becomes of their dupes as long as their own coffers are filled, and who have studied the most attractive means to remove any objection to the section they pretend to represent that may be raised by those who are opposed to emigrating. They represent to the lazy and indolent that, by emigrating to their chosen spot they will find a country so favored by nature, and in which the spontaneous productions of the soil are so varied and bountiful, as to preclude the necessity of labor, and to the more grasping and avaricious they represent that a fortune is in store for them, and when acquired they will be enabled to successfully establish themselves where they please. These two classes of persons are of little, if any, use anywhere, and can be very well spared from our own "Sunny South"; but there is another class that is being induced to leave us, who will, if they remain [here], contribute largely by their energy and industry in doing all that can be done towards re-establishing us in a condition of independence, and to a great extent recuperate our now shattered fortunes.

It is this latter portion of our people that we desire should remain, and not be led astray by the "wolf in sheep's clothing." It cannot be questioned that at this time the whole country is in a condition of greater pecuniary prostration than we have ever before realized, and that our section seems to have reached so low a point as almost to have passed the limit that will justify the hope of recuperation; yet we are satisfied "when things get to their worst they generally improve," and in this reflection there is room for a little hope, if not for great buoyancy of spirits. It is to be regretted that the time of improvement in our circumstances is in the dim and distant future; so far, indeed, that we are unable to penetrate the gloom by which we are surrounded, and through which there is scarcely a gleam of light to direct us on our way. The work of a people in recuperating their condition after such losses as we have sustained, in a financial point of view only, must necessarily be slow, and require time for its consummation; but with us it can safely be said there is no foundation on which to build, or at least it is of such a character as to prevent our rearing a superstructure that will promise durability and satisfaction.

We are deprived of our former labor system, that enabled us to increase our worldly possessions and enrich the North, and are now compelled to depend upon a system of labor that prevents the possibility of our raising our great staple productions at a price that will prove remunerating. Our cotton, that at one time enabled us to contribute so much towards defraying the expenses of the Government, can do so no longer, and those who have been engaged in its cultivation since the war, must discontinue it, as loss has attended nearly every effort to produce it by our own people who were acquainted with the plant, and a like want of success has attended the trials made by those who have come from other sections, and who knew but little of its cultivation, and whose capital was the only advantage they possessed over us. Again, it is well known that Europe no longer looks to this country for its supply of cotton, and that we have lost control of the cotton markets of the world, which was not the case before the war. We are without capital, and very few are willing to invest their means in our section during the present disturbed condition of our affairs.

The destruction of our great planting interests has reduced us to a consuming, instead of being, as formerly, a producing people, and we cannot expect for a long time to come that we will occupy any other position. The history of the world produces sufficient evidence by the experience of all who have gone before us, that a people to be prosperous must have the balance of trade in their favor, or at least there should not be such a difference as at present exists between ourselves and the rest of the world. If we cannot raise the staples it was formerly our custom to produce in such quantity, and at such price as to enable us to govern the markets that required them for consumption, it may be well to ask what we can raise. There can be no doubt of our ability to produce all, or nearly all we may require to subsist upon, but what can we raise for export, and thereby prevent the excessive balance of trade being against us that we know, to have been the case during the past three years? The question is more easily asked than answered. The successful cultivation of the soil will insure prosperity in every business and pursuit, and a failure will produce a corresponding or proportionate depression in every occupation the human family is engaged in. Although we have a climate as genial as any on earth, and a soil as rich, we must come to the unfortunate conclusion that our agricultural pursuits must languish for a time, and during that time we must remain a consuming people, and consequently be poorer to-day than we were yesterday.

For every evil there is a remedy, if we only know how and when to apply it, and all who read these pages are as capable of applying it as myself, and it is hoped, more so****** These thoughts are suggested by the fact of our having been almost entirely engaged in planting, and but comparatively little in manufacturing, and show plainly how poor we have become as a people. This condition causes many to look about them to endeavor to fix upon some spot where they may have a more favorable prospect of making a living than at present seems to be the case here. The primary cause of the dissatisfaction of our people, and the cause of every evil we are now subjected to is, the political atmosphere of the country, and no apparent prospect of its changing for the better at an early day. We are politically nothing—taxed beyond precedent—denied representation—almost deprived of the ability to pay taxes, and without a voice in the formation of those laws by which we are to be governed—the party in power striving by every means in its power to place an inferior race in a position of political importance, and to even elevate to social equality a people it was undoubtedly the intention of our Creator should occupy a position below us, and be under our direction as certainly as it was His intention that the superiors should control the inferior.

This is a gloomy array of evils, and should it not rather cause us to buckle on our armor and to make a powerful effort to keep this country under the control of the white men? There are thousands of our friends who must permanently abide here, come weal or come woe; and should we not feel it incumbent upon us to remain and engage in that political contest for supremacy which must come sooner or later, and perhaps at an early day? A struggle that will be more fiercely contested than any we have gone through when the sullen boom of artillery, the rattle of musketry, and the dying groans of our friends and relatives were heard—a contest fraught with more momentous issues than it has ever been the duty of a nation before to engage in, as it will settle the question whether we are to be slaves or freemen—whether we are to be governed by intelligence, or by an ignorant population, whose principal idea of liberty seems to be that it consists in the removal of every restraint, the absence of all law. Let us make a determined effort to save the old ship that has weathered so many storms, and is now in the breakers, and in danger of being dashed to pieces, and not say we care not who is at the helm, or how fiercely the storm rages. If, after using every means at our command, the vessel is wrecked, we may then seize a plank and trust to the Giver of all Good to waft us to a harbor of safety.

What have we yet done to check the current that seems hurrying us to destruction? Nothing, simply nothing; and the idea that we are too weak, is too feeble an argument for men to use who have undergone what we have from 1861 to the present time. What we have done since the close of the war has encouraged the radical party to make greater demands than they would have thought of making, but for our concessions from time to time.

We have taken counsel from our fears, and have done too much through policy, a fruit that has a most inviting exterior, but within is bitter indeed. Let us in future claim all we feel we are entitled to, and contend for it with all our power; again I say let us do our duty, and if we are overtaken and overpowered, let every true and honored southron [sic] be prepared to exclaim, "Shake not thy gory locks at me; thou can'st not say I did it," and let him gather together the fragments he may have saved from the wreck, leave the home of his childhood, the graves of his kindred, and seek some land where he may have the satisfaction of rearing his children in the midst of those who have feelings common with them, and with whom they may associate on terms of equality. We have sacrificed nearly our entire property in the vain endeavor to better our condition; and let us show to the world our willingness to make other and greater sacrifices, but not to the end that radicalism shall rule this land—the fairest of earth, and surrender to those who are in every way unfitted to occupy it, the heritage of our fathers.

No, rather than this should be, better, far better that this land should sink, and that waves of ocean should roll over what was once a happy and a prosperous country—that the map of the world should show no spot once occupied by our territory—our names be a myth—our requiem be the howling winds and the roaring waves, and our dirge the scream of the gull in his passage over our ruined homes and unknown graves. Better far better that all save honor and the immortal soul should be lost, than that party whose motto seems to be equality, in every sense in which it can be used, should prevail. We can accomplish something, and let us do what we can; and if we fail, we will have the proud consolation of knowing we made every effort to keep our country in the enviable position it has hitherto occupied among the nations of the earth. If despite our exertions to the contrary, our country should be brought to the humiliating fact of equality of races existing among us—when an inferior holds public position, and even serves in the capacity of representatives of the people, or when we are satisfied this will be the result of what is now transpiring, it will be well to surrender this land to our persecutors, and time will make known whether they have acted well or wisely. Let each and every one do what seemeth unto him best, keeping in view the fact that there is still a duty for all to perform, and which should be accomplished, if possible, regardless of what the consequences may be. We have work to do not for ourselves only, but for generations yet unborn, and who will hardly think of us with veneration if we fail to exert ourselves in this in a manner commensurate with the importance of the questions involved. It may be too late to accomplish good, but it can never be too late to make the attempt. Under certain circumstances it will be seen I favor emigration and this may be the most favorable time for such a movement. At all events, I shall, on my return from Belize, publish all the information gathered in that country, and if it serves as a guide to even one in the formation of an opinion as to what is best to be done, some little good may be accomplished.

It is my intention to get information from the most reliable sources, and to describe as nearly as possible what is seen, and as the trip is not for purposes of speculation, I hope to be able to give a correct, though condensed account of what distant land in every particular that promises to be of project to those who contemplate making it their future residence. * * * * * *

This is the land of my birth and where I had hoped to be able to live in the peaceful enjoyment of my own. It has been my desire here to be buried, and that my ashes might mingle with those of my kindred, but it may be otherwise ordained, and be my lot to repose in a land far distant from the scenes of my childhood; and if so, I will cast the anchor of hope in such waters as my destiny may waft me to, ever trusting in Him who "doeth all things well," to carry me safely through my earthly pilgrimage and finally to a haven of eternal rest.

Warren Co., Miss., October 7th, 1867

BRITISH HONDURAS

DECEMBER 26th—Our party, according to agreement, left "old Warren" this morning by rail for Belize, via New Orleans, though two of our number remain behind and will follow by the next steamer, if we do not give such a representation on our arrival at our point of destination, as to make it unnecessary for them to come, as we can write by return of steamer, being informed she lies at Belize several days. We reached New Orleans in safety, at 8 A.M., and are now located at the St. Charles.[2] Never before have I had such feelings as possess me at this time. I know not how to express them. It

---

2. The St. Charles Hotel was the venerable hostelry of choice for planters, prominent business-people, and wealthy travelers. In the words of an article that appeared in the April 30, 1894, issue of the *New York Times*, the St. Charles was "For Nearly Sixty years a Centre of Southern Social and Political Life." For additional information about the hotel, see John Kendall, *History of New Orleans* (Chicago: Lewis Publishing, 1922), 685–692.

is certainly nothing new for me to be absent from home, the late war having necessitated that from its beginning to its end, with the exception of a few days; but this trip oppresses me with feelings of sadness. What am I about to do? To leave my native land, it is hoped, for a short time but to engage in a tour of observation for the benefit, I trust, of many, but not with the desire or intention to influence any.

Not having inaugurated this expedition, as stated in my prefatory remarks, and representing others, it is my earnest wish to give a clear and unvarnished statement of all I see, and all that is heard from reliable sources, ever preferring an occular demonstration, when possible, to representations of any one, not because of a want of confidence in my fellow man, or fear of being deceived, feeling satisfied that such letters as we carry will place us properly before the officials, but because such information can not fail to be of a more gratifying character to those who desire facts, intermingled with no portion of fiction. In the morning our party will proceed to get together such articles as we may need for the trip, not trusting to our getting anything at Belize.

DECEMBER 27th.—To-day was spent in completing our outfit, and in obtaining letters, in which latter undertaking we were very much assisted by General B. [Beauregard?], who secured for us an introduction to the British Consul, and a letter from him direct to his Excellency the Governor of [British] Honduras.

DECEMBER 28th—Not having quite completed our arrangements on yesterday, we are making a finish to-day, and must be on shipboard by 5 P.M., according to advertisement, though there is no absolute necessity for hurry on that account, as they are known not to be quite as punctual as the sun. Our purchases being completed, and on board at 4 o'clock, we left the hotel for the steamer Trade-Wind, expecting to be in the gulf before morning. The vessel was ready to sail by 7 o'clock, but a dense fog rising, we lay at the pier all night, much to our disappointment, as we are anxious to get forward as rapidly as possible, but we must accept the situation as additional evidence of the fallibility of human calculation, which we can safely do without fear of being opposed by this cloud of vapor for any length of time. Would we could say as much of that cloud which obscures in its sable folds our political horizon, and now seems threatening to veil the star of hope with its funereal pall; the first produces not a disagreeable sensation of chilliness, but the latter penetrating the inmost recesses of the heart and causing a degree of cold that cannot be removed by any ordinary means.

DECEMBER 29th.—This morning we find ourselves still at the pier, but not without hope of being able to get off in an hour or two. The fog disappearing at 7.45 A.M., we left our moorings and many now consider ourselves on our way. This being Sunday, we had Divine Service; the Rev. Mr. Morrill, of Texas, preaching, who although over sixty years of age, is on his way to a new country, and though in feeble health, does not fear to brave any hardship he may have to encounter, or any privation he may be called upon to suffer. In the evening we had a discourse from the Rev. Mr. Pearce, of Mississippi, who is on board with his family, and goes for the purpose of locating, though he has never seen the country.

His faith and determination cannot but be admired, though I confess that it would require more than the writer ever had or ever expects to possess, to induce a move of the same kind. It is perhaps best that the Pioneer should sever every connection with his former home, and then, if dissatisfied with a new country at first, he will remain and eventually become reconciled to those customs and things that at first made an unfavorable impression, and might have induced a departure from a land that promised less than was expected. To-day has been gloomy, with rain, which increased as the day advanced, and as we came to anchor, just inside the bar, there is every appearance of a storm. Here we must lay till morning; it being impossible to go over the bar to-night.

Our careful commander informs us it is possible we may have to remain at our anchorage for several hours in the morning.

DECEMBER 30th.—This morning it is cloudy, cool and windy, and our captain has determined to remain till the middle of the day, if the weather does not sooner improve; he represents the outside to be pretty rough, with the wind in its present direction. There are many on board who would prefer smooth water, and though they were anxious to leave the Crescent City, and have shown some impatience at each delay, are now willing to abide by the decision of one who has the reputation of being an excellent seaman; all fearing sea-sickness, which is anything but agreeable, those who have experienced its effects state that when under its influence is the best possible time for a man to take his departure to the land of spirits, and a person suffering from it will not unfrequently request to be rolled overboard, with the view of trying the water cure. We trust our knowledge of it may be confined to what we have heard, not feeling anxious to verify those statements. By the way, we have been told by the initiated, it is not a bad plan to take a little spirits, to prevent nausea. Not having tried it, can say nothing of its efficacy, but we can all add our testimony to the fact that the prescription is not a bad one, and having a supply of the medicine with us, it is not improbable we may try it. We have also been informed that champagne is very good for the same purpose, but as our finances are not in as healthy a condition as in former days, as "Bill Arp" said, when asked what state he lived in, "The less we say about that the better."[3]

At 11 o'clock, the wind having died away, and our pilot being on board, we weighed anchor and again pursued our way to the South-West pass, through which we make our entrance to the Gulf. We found a heavy sea outside, which soon caused sea-sickness with most of those who were for the first time being tossed upon the "briny deep." The writer was one of the first to succumb, notwithstanding the remedy above spoken of, and the most powerful exercise of the will in connection. There was no wish for the table during that day or the next, or the next, and the dinner bell was even resorted to with no effect.

It is perhaps well enough to state here, that those who contemplate making a sea voyage for the first time should be thoroughly impressed with the fact that they are about to leave home, and home comforts, and shou'd prepare themselves in every way possible to meet the exigencies that may arise, and not trust to obtaining them on shipboard, as those who have control of vessels are acted upon by the same influences that control persons in other situations in life, and feel that to provide for themselves is the first step, and, perhaps, with too many the last that should be taken. Let all be provided with such simple medicines as they are in the habit of using at home, with lemons, or sugar of lemon, which is very convenient, spoons, mugs, crushed sugar, ale or porter, and a small quantity of such liquors and wine as they may prefer; feeling satisfied that by such means much suffering will be prevented: and even should the articles not be used and it should be necessary to throw them away, the loss can not be great. Five gallons of water and, if possible, some ice, would not be out of place in a voyage from New Orleans to Belize.

DECEMBER 31st.—The weather is cloudy, and with a good breeze and steam, we are making very good headway, and we earnestly hope to make a quick trip. Very few persons are able to be about, nearly all being confined to their berths. We have over one hundred passengers on board, with quite

---

3. Bill Arp was the pseudonym of Charles Henry Smith, a Georgia lawyer who wrote humorous and extremely popular pro-Confederate essays during the Civil War.

a number of ladies and children among them, and when mother and child are both sick, the poor little one sadly feels the loss of the parent's soothing influences.

JANUARY 1.—We are still tossed upon the waves and very few are in condition to eat a New Year's dinner, if within reach, but nothing is heard of any such preparation. For a time, though we are to be separated from our homes, and to be surrounded by a waste of waters, which we may not inappropriately consider emblematic of the present condition of our unfortunate and oppressed South, which seems separate from the world, and to occupy no political position, and which is lashed by angry political waters which threaten the destruction of the old Ship of State, we are united in our determination to carve out for our friends and selves some plan by which we may have a voice in the "laws by which we are governed," though of course we cannot expect to act in that direction any further than to give evidence of what will promote our welfare, and trust to the kindness of those in whose midst we may be, to feel and to exercise sufficient charity toward us, to cause them, in some measure, to provide for our political wants.

JANUARY 2.—We find in our little vessel many gentlemen from Louisiana, Arkansas, Mississippi and from other Southern States, who before the war were in affluent circumstances, and consequently removed from the necessity of performing any kind of manual labor, now express their willingness to do as far as they are able, whatever may be necessary to enable them to make a support for themselves and families. We have a most excellent list of passengers, and have been very fortunate in forming a party for exploration, consisting of some of the best men it has ever been our fortune to meet with. All seem firmly impressed with the necessity for a change, and the determination they evince, and the willingness they express to combat any hardship they may have to encounter, and to overcome all obstacles that may be presented, is a pretty good evidence that success is likely to attend their efforts, or at least affords us reasonable hope that such will be the final result.

JANUARY 3.—The weather still continues somewhat cloudy which is fortunate for us, as the temperature is lower in consequence, though we have at no time since leaving New Orleans found it as high as in that city. Indeed, though we are approaching the equator, the remarkable fact has impressed all, that the heat is less oppressive from day to day. Tomorrow we should be at Belize, but the prospect now is that we will not reach our destination before the next day. Patience is a virtue, but all are extremely anxious to get where more freedom of locomotion may be enjoyed.

JANUARY 4.—To-day the hitherto unbroken and monotonous blank has been broken by the appearance of land, and all are cheered by the sight, and now feel satisfied this is the last day of our voyage, which has already extended to a greater length than any of us could have wished. Before leaving our homes, we were informed the trip would occupy four days; by the time we reach New Orleans, five days, which by the time we reached the mouth of the river had extended to six, and our unfortunate experience is that seven are required; at least such has been the time on our passage, we having cast anchor this evening, at about 6 o'clock, off the town of Belize, British Honduras, and step number one may now fairly be considered terminated.

Before leaving the scene I feel it to be my duty to speak in terms of praise of our purser, Col. Harney, who is an ex-confederate, and a whole-souled, liberal gentleman; and of Mr. Scoville, chief engineer of the boat, through whose kindness we were supplied with one of the best rooms on the vessel, he having with a spirit of liberality and self-denial rarely witnessed these days of selfishness, resigned to our use his own room, thereby subjecting himself to inconvenience, but we sincerely hope, not to discomfort. May he never feel the want of a friend, and may his pilgrimage through life be attended with as few obstructions as fall to the lot of man. We will ever hold him in grateful remembrance. We are all anxious to get ashore to-night, but having made earnest efforts to do so, and failing, must rest content till morning. One thing is consoling, however, we are in smooth water, compared with what we have passed over, and the vessel being still, have the prospect of a good night's rest, which will be worth something to us, and indeed is much needed by all.

JANUARY 5.—We succeeded in getting ashore this morning by 9 o'clock, and finding no hotel for our accommodation, fortunately made arrangements with Mr. Mahler, an old resident of the place, to provide for our wants, which he did during our stay here, in good style; taking the house formerly occupied for the same purpose by Mr. Ware. From this location we have a beautiful view of the Bay, and have nothing in front to obstruct the breeze, which is truly delightful.

BELIZE, FROM THE LANDING.

6. City of Belize. E. G. Squier, *The States of Central America* (New York: Harper & Brothers, 1858), 574.

JANUARY 6.—To-day we have an opportunity of looking around us, and must say our impressions of Belize, from report, have been very different from the reality. We find a very well built town of about 7000 inhabitants, and doing a very considerable business. The houses are mostly one story, but we give hereafter a full description of the place and its surroundings.

Insertion, pp. 77–80 in original

It is singular, but true, that few persons who have not visited Belize, have any well defined or correct ideas of that place. Of all the passengers on the Tradewind when we went over, there being more than a hundred, only two or three persons, who had visited the country, had any other idea of the place than that the houses were rudely constructed, and the principal portion of the population about as rude as buildings. We confess our surprise was great, when first we caught sight of the town, at night, but greater was our surprise when we viewed it in the morning, and found that it extended along the shore for a distance of more than a mile with well built houses and palm trees scattered here and there, waving their umbrella like tops to the breeze, and relieving the monotonous white of the buildings by their foliage, presenting a very beautiful and fairy-like scene.

The town has a width of less than half of mile, with a Mangrove swamp extending along its rear, and is drained by the Belize River, which places the northern end in an island made by the water of the river passing through the "haul over" six miles from town. There is a canal running the entire length of the place, and in rear of it, which is twenty-five feet wide, piled on either side, and spanned by several iron bridges. The streets are of good width, without sidewalks and are kept scrupulously clean. No matter how hard it may rain or how windy it may be, there is no mud in the one case, nor dust in the other, as the streets are made of sand and small gravel, and are so hard and smooth as to present the appearance of cement or concrete walks.

The Customhouse is an excellent building, and has a beautiful wharf, close by; the market house, though not large, is constructed of iron, and the bridge which spans the river is a very substantial structure, though built of wood. The houses are from one to three stories high, and are constructed of brick, frame, and a few of corrugated iron; and are covered principally with slate, tile and iron. Most persons do business on the lower floor and reside above, where may be found apartments as neatly constructed and as elegantly furnished as at any other place we can name. The merchants of Belize are able to drive their business, and not let their business drive them, for at 4 o'clock P.M. every store of any pretensions is closed, with a promptness that caused us to ask if it was in accordance with law, and were informed it was simply a custom. (Happy merchants, thought we, if you do not do business on twelve months' time. If you lived in the United States you would think slavery still in existence, as with us there is certainly no class of men who are worked harder than the merchants.)

There are six churches; two Episcopal, one Methodist, one Baptist, one Catholic and one Presbyterian. All very neat and large for a place the size of Belize; the Methodist being very handsome indeed. We will endeavor to give a short description of it. The corner stone was laid by Gov. Austin, November 3d, 1864. The building is constructed of brick, with slate roof, and covers a surface of about 50X100 feet, and has two floors, the lower one with ceiling about fifteen feet high, which is used as a school-room, and the upper for Divine service; a stair-case running from the outside of the building, being the mode of reaching it. The pews are of Mahogany, and the pulpit is of the same material; large, and circular in form, with a handsome lamp on either side of the cushion and two in the rear. In rear of the pulpit are three tablets, six feet high and three in width, those at the sides containing the Ten Commandments, and that in the centre the Apostles Creed. Gothic windows of green glass occupy nearly the entire width of the building, at the end where the pulpit is situated, and on either side of the room double gothic windows of colored glass, with circular windows above them, extend from floor to ceiling, which is a gothic vault, with a base one half the width of the building, and from which two arches gracefully curve to the walls. The ceiling is painted white, and is relieved by strips of mahogany, several inches wide, running from base to apex, at intervals of about three feet. Five chandeliers with three lights each, are suspended from the roof, and eight lamps at the walls, four on either side. We found by calculation that the floor would hold four hundred and fifty-six persons, and the gallery one hundred and eight.

We attended service here at night, two hundred or more of the colored population being present, and only *three white persons*, that we could see, and we never saw a more quiet or attentive congregation. The moment we appeared at the door, we were politely conducted to a seat, and every attention shown that could anywhere be given.

There is considerable business done at Belize, though we are inclined to think from the appearance of stocks in store that too heavy a preparation has been made for the immigrants' accommodation. There are few roads around the town, and not many in the country generally, transportation being carried on with boats and pack mules. A boat is almost as indispensable to an inhabitant of this place as a carriage or buggy is with us, and they seem to have exhausted their skill and ingenuity in the construction—some of them being very artistically and elegantly made. There are several kinds of boats, the most important being the "Dorey" and "Pitpan." The first is shaped like a ship's boat, and sharp at both ends, and the second is very long for its width and is used for navigating shallow water. These boats are made of a single piece of wood, and are what we would call "canoes, or dug-outs."

End of Insertion

JANUARY 6th. [Continued] We to-day formed a party for purposes of exploration, consisting of the following gentlemen who were passengers on the Trade Wind:

Rev. Levi Pearce. . . . . of Sharon, Mississippi.
Col. J. E. F. Harrison . . . . of Tenses, Louisiana.
Dan'l. Swett . . . . of Vicksburg, Miss.
Dr. G. P. Frierson. . . . . of DeSoto, Louisiana
Dr. G. A. Frierson . . . . " "
Dr. R. F. Gray . . . . of Opelousas, "
Capt. W. Buckner . . . . of Tensas, "
J. S. Peak . . . . of Chicot, Arkansas

E. V. Frierson . . . . of DeSoto, Louisiana
T. C. Frierson. . . . . " "
T. F. Owen . . . . of Catahoula, "
Thos. P. Kane . . . . of Jackson,"
T. P. Morris. . . . . of Batesville, Arkansas.
Chas. Swett. . . . . of Warren Co., Miss.

and last, though not an unimportant personage, Wm. Owens, an "American citizen of African descent," who accompanies Col. H. to serve him in the capacity of cook, being an old servant of the Colonel. We today visited Mr. Jas. M. Putnam, formerly of the U.S., and who is at present acting as agent for the firm of Messrs. Young, Toledo & Co., of Belize, in the sale of their lands, and through his kindness received an introduction to Messrs. McDonald and Harrison, who are in charge of the very business of the firm at this place. Our interview was very pleasant, and we found these gentlemen ready to grant every facility in their power to enable us to carry to a successful issue, the objects of our mission. We were also introduced by Mr. P. to Mr. Mathe, with whom we spent a very pleasant hour in the evening, and obtained from him some very interesting facts connected with his experience as a sugar planter, which we regret to say has thus far not proved very profitable.

JANUARY 7th.—Having letters to Gov. Longdon, we called upon his excellency today, being accompanied by Mr. P., and were very kindly received. While we were not discouraged by the interview, we can say that Gov. Longdon did not at once accept as fact the many reports concerning the great agricultural and planting properties of the Colony, but gave us every reason to believe that what could be done by the government, in conformity with its laws, to promote the welfare of emigrants, would be done, but at the same time would offer no extraordinary inducements to emigrants. Some of our party believing that they could become British Subjects, in its most extended sense, were informed by his excellency, that after they had selected the country as their place of residence, should they make application for letters of naturalization, they would be granted, but they would only entitle the recipient to colonial protection, while in the colony, and not to the protection of the British Government when removed beyond the limits of the Colony. Some were much disappointed at this, as they had hoped by becoming citizens they would secure to themselves the guardian care of certainly the best government on earth, wherever they might be, so long as they claimed their home in British Honduras.

Insertion, pp. 85–86 in original

. . . [I]t is a pleasure to add our testimony to the fact that his Excellency, Jas. Robt. Longdon, Governor of British Honduras is a gentleman in every way qualified for the position he fills with so much satisfaction to the people of the colony, and that he possesses the rare combination of an excellent administrative and executive officer, the result of large experience and close observation, which, together with a finished education, polished manner, and earnest desire to promote the welfare of those under him has greatly endeared him to all.

We found him also to be eminently practical in his ideas, and trust if this should meet his eye, that he will excuse our using an expression made use of by him, and which we not soon forget, "that he did not so much desire to hear what persons could do, as what they had accomplished" in their planting operations.

End of Insertion

JANUARY 8th.—Being busy to-day in completing our preparations to explore the bush, we again called in requisition the aid of our friend, Mr. Putnam, who is ever ready to assist all who visit [British] Honduras to an extent that has, and will continue to trespass heavily upon his time, though he seems able to, or at least does, the work of about three men. Having deemed it best to do so, have secured a schooner, by charter, to convey us to any point we may desire to visit, and for an indefinite length of time. Our party being divided into committees, in order to facilitate business, we hope to be off tomorrow. Since our arrival here, the breeze has been constantly blowing very freshly from the bay, and at night were lulled to sleep by its sighing through the lattice, the sound would alternately rise to Eolian sweetness, and almost die away, which was peculiarly grateful to the feelings, and far from being unpleasant to the ear; but what pleasure was ever unalloyed, or continued for any length of time without interruption? The wind entirely died away at 8 o'clock this evening, and before ten changed to the north-west, causing an invasion of our premises by such a force of *sand flies* as to render opposition futile, and we were punished to a degree that it is impossible for us to make known, but will ever be remembered; being entirely without bars, except the writer, who was supplied with one made this morning, of muslin, but at the moment out of reach because needed. Suffice it to say for the present that, they give no notice of their approach, came in immense force, and each individual armed with what seemed to us to be a red-hot needle, which they used with a vigor worthy of a better cause, and served to admonish the poor "ex-confeds" that it was still their destiny to suffer.

JANUARY 9th.—This morning the wind is blowing from the opposite direction, sand flies are gone, and we will endeavor to forget the miseries of the past night, and more particularly, as we have determined not to be checked by any obstacle or annoyance we may meet with, but to battle cheerfully every opposing cause in striving for the end we wish to attain. Although we had fully expected to make a start this morning, the very disagreeable information is imparted to us that the vessel chartered yesterday can not go, and we are under the necessity of getting another. Fortunately, a schooner is in port from Omoa, which we have engaged, and which is now unloading, therefore can reasonably expect to leave Belize in the distance to-morrow, at furthest. It would have been better had we visited the schooner before chartering her, but we did not, yet feel it our duty to make the following statement, in the hope it may be of some service to those who may hereafter be situated as we were. Between Omoa and Belize a considerable trade is carried on in swine, by means of schooners varying in capacity from ten to fifty tons, the animals being placed in the hold of the vessel. The schooner selected by us had just arrived with a cargo of this description, and though an attempt was made at cleansing, it became very apparent in the course of a day that the process might have been carried to much greater extent, with decided advantage.

JANUARY 10th.—At 9 this morning we started for the schooner "Three Sisters," of 11 tons, Capt. Francisco Solaro, which was anchored about half a mile from shore, though the Captain and crew did not come aboard till 2:45 P.M., when we weighed anchor for Manatee Bar, eighteen miles distant, and a little west of south from Belize. The pilot who was to accompany us, came on board with the Captain, but without his knowing it returned in the boat that brought them off. After sailing a mile, we came to anchor, and Capt. Solaro returned to Belize to investigate the conduct of the pilot. Being pleasantly located, and a delightful breeze blowing from the north-west, must exercise patience, our stocks of which we did not find excessive, as requisition has to be made in that direction very frequently, for very large quantities, to be delivered in the very best order, and immediately. At 3.45 the Captain returned without the pilot and we again weighed anchor and proceeded on our way without that individual, although we feel the necessity of having one, as our captain does not know all the points we desire to visit. Having heard much of Spanish Honduras during our few days stay at Belize, several of our party desire to visit that country, whatever may be the result of our present trip, as it will occupy but a few days to do so, and we can then verify or disprove by occular demonstration the extravagant stories we have heard of the Republic. Thermometer, F. 6 A.M., 72; 12 M., 82 1-2; 6 P.M., 82 1-2.

JANUARY 11th.—Finding that we could not reach Manatee Bar before night, in consequence of our late start, have concluded to go on, and visit it on our return. At a reasonable hour at night we disposed ourselves for sleep; the older gentlemen occupying the four berths of the cabin, others taking the hold of the vessel, and some using their hammocks, slung in the rigging: ourself and one other taking the top of the cabin, which was elevated a few feet above deck. At 12 all on deck were aroused by a shower, delivered by a passing cloud, and which cooled the atmosphere to such an extent as to make two blankets decidedly comfortable, and of course one each was the extent of our supply in that direction. As for the wetting we received, our experience in that way has been too extensive in time past to give it a passing thought. It being so very cool we examined the thermometer and to our astonishment found it to indicate 83 degrees, although there is no breeze, and our vessel is drifting with the current. This remarkable difference between actual, and from one's feelings, apparent temperature, we will revert to again when on the subject of climate.

JANUARY 11th.—At 6 A.M. we were very near the mouth of North Stann Creek, distant thirty-five miles from Belize, and made for it in order to go ashore. At 7 we cast anchor, and visited a Carib village located here, which we found to extend along the coast for the distance of half a mile, and to contain about 800 inhabitants, and a methodist and a catholic church. Mr. Brown, the police officer of the place, was absent, as was also the methodist minister; therefore, we passed through the village and trusted to our observation for information. We found the houses to be built about square, eighteen feet the usual size, and to be constructed of studding, with cane of the country secured across them, and filled with clay; the roof being very steep, forming an equilateral triangle, and being covered with the split branches of the Cahoon palm. They have no chimneys, no windows with glass, nor floors, except those made of "mother earth." We here saw the manner in which the Cassava root is prepared for bread. (See description of that root.) The root is grated and placed in a long tube, or bag, five feet in length and four inches in diameter, which is suspended from a beam till all sap of the root is drained from it, when it is sifted, made into cakes which are two feet in diameter, and one fourth of an inch thick, and baked. This is called Cassava, or pilot bread, and will keep a very long time; has a cream color, but though we have eaten much of it, do not think we would prefer it, under any circumstances, to the wheaten loaf or the corn cake of our country.

Their graters and sifters we deem worthy of description, and are made as follows. The grater is a piece of mahogany 1¼ inches thick, 18 inches wide and 2½ feet long, across which lines are drawn three-fourths of an inch apart, which lines are divided along their length so that the division lines will run diagonally, and at each point of division a hole is punched and a pice [*sic*] of broken pebble driven in that will not be more than half the size of a pea, and the grater is complete. The sifter is 3 feet in diameter, and is made of split cane, through which the Cassava is rubbed by the hands, and not by shaking as with us. From eight to ten miles in rear of this place, though the distance does not appear so great, there is a range of high hills. The natives plant at and near the base of these, and depend upon the Belize market for the sale of all they have to dispose of. The coast is not more than two feet above the level of the sea, the waters of which are well stocked with fish, if we can rely upon the statements of the natives.

We also saw quite a quantity of fish drying across poles. We here found a dory, made of Spanish cedar, which measured 36 feet in length, 7 feet wide, 3 feet deep, 1½ inches thick and elegantly modeled. After purchasing some oranges at 75 cents per hundred, we returned to the vessel and at 9.20 A.M. weighed anchor for "All Pines," forty-five miles distant from Belize. The natives of the village just left were found to be polite, and willingly answered any questions we propounded, though they frequently manifested some surprise at our ignorance of their manners and customs, and would laugh heartily at our description of the customs of our own country, and the differences that existed among us. They could all speak English, and we therefore had no difficulty in making ourselves understood. Cocoa nuts, oil from the cocoa nut, and oranges was all they offered for sale.

On being asked why the oil was so white and thick, they replied, "it is because the weather is so cold!" The thermometer at the time ranging as high as 76 degrees. There being very little breeze, we did not reach "All Pines" till 2.25 P.M., where we immediately went ashore for the purpose of visiting one of the sugar estates of Mr. Mathé. We found Mr. Debraam, whose residence is on the coast, immediately on landing, who received us very cordially, and expressed his regret that he could not furnish us with conveyance to the estate, three miles distant, that evening, there being too many of us to accommodate thus far, on the limited notice given him, and as we were anxious to keep moving, at once proceeded on foot for the "Estate."

For one-half the distance from the coast to the "Estate" we found the country at the time it was opened to have been covered with pine, most of which had been made into lumber and sent to the West Indies by Mr. Deb-raam. There is quite a large store near the coast, a very complete lumber mill, and a foundry, the property of the Estate. Over the distance between these two points is a most excellent road, which, for about half the way has been thrown up, at great expense, in order to avoid the mud of the wet season. The Estates, there being three in number, and not very far apart, Mr. Debraam superintends the whole, which are situated on the "Sittee" river, and twelve miles from the coast by water though only three by land.

On our way up we saw many cattle, though they did not look so well as we had reason to expect in this land of perpetual pasturage. Mr. Aquet, Mr. Savage and Mr. Hanson, who are in charge of different duties on the premises, very kindly gave us all the information we desired. What we here witnessed would certainly astonish a Louisiana sugar planter. The places were opened in 1863, and Mr. Debraam informed us he expected to make six thousand pounds of sugar per acre, and there being four hundred acres in cultivation, it is a question for the juveniles to decide how much coffee it will sweeten. A gentleman of our party who is well acquainted with the production of sugar, when told of the expectation as to yield, looked incredulous, but after making an examination of the growing crop, remarked that he was prepared to believe ten thousand pounds could be made to the acre if the yield should prove in proportion to the quantity of cane produced, taking the Louisiana yield as his basis.

Plenty of the canes were two and a half inches in diameter and fifteen to twenty feet in length. The fields were a perfect mass of vegetation, the canes growing to a certain height, and under their own weight falling over and again growing up, forming curves not unlike the letter S [on its side] when in this position. Many of us were at first disappointed because of the cane not growing higher, and one of our party caught hold of a top which was not more than three feet above the ground, and asked one of the gentlemen in charge of the place if he called that sugar cane; at the same time giving it a jerk, when it developed the fact that three feet was not its length, but eighteen, which proved satisfactory to all parties concerned.

The buildings on the place are not constructed of brick, and might be more properly called sheds, though constructed in the most substantial manner, with galvanized corrugated iron roofing, and the machinery of the most costly and approved patterns. A very large sum has been expended, and thus far no return for the outlay of capital. No plows are used in preparing the ground, but holes are dug with a hoe or machete, in rows six feet apart and three inches to one foot in length, and when once planted it is said to rattoon for fifteen years, and has been known to do so for a greater length of time. The best time for planting the cane is in October and November, though it may be planted at any time during the rainy season—which is said to begin about the first of June and to continue to the end of the year.

The grinding is commenced in from twelve to fourteen months, notwithstanding the statements that have appeared in print that two and three crops can be made in a year. Having made use of the word "Machete" for the first time, and its being an indispensable article in this country, it is well to describe it here as elsewhere. (It is a heavy knife, from eighteen to twenty-four inches in length, and from two to two and a half inches in width, with a proportionate thickness, and is to the native, his axe, his hatchet, his saw, his plow, harrow, shovel, spade, hoe, pruning knife and weapon of defense. They never go to the woods without it, and we have seen them cut asunder logs eight and ten inches in diameter with them, though of course the implement would have been broken in the hand of one of less experience.) We measured at "All Pines" a Dorey that is perhaps the largest in [British] Honduras. It is thirty-five feet long, eight feet wide and four feet deep, and is to receive machinery that will weigh two tuns [sic], and be used between this point and Belize for the benefit of the "Estates."

On reaching the schooner, all were very tired, having walked continually since leaving the vessel, though we have all been amply repaid for the investment of physical exertion, for it can safely be said we have had occular demonstration of at least one of the wonders of this said to be wonderful portion of the earth. Our next place of landing will be South Stann Creek, fifty miles from Belize, and it being close by, have determined to lay here tonight and make an early start in the morning. Thermometer 6 A.M. 75 1-2; 12 M. 81; 6 P.M. 80 1-2.

JANUARY 12th—We weighed anchor at 5 A.M., and again cast anchor at South Stann Creek, near the residence of Mr. C. Chamberlin, who has a large body of land at this point, purchased of Mr. Mathé. Mr. C. formerly resided at Natchez, and though he has been in possession of a large property, had his family living within reach of every luxury of life, and is now in possession of a much larger portion of this world's goods than is the case with most of us, this gentleman, with an elegant and accomplished family, reared in luxury, has chosen to lead the life of a pioneer in a comparatively unknown country, where law and order prevail, rather than to remain in a land where there is but little protection, and less prospect of accumulation. May they reap the reward of their determination, enterprise and self-denial. Mr. C. having been here for a very short time, has made very little clearing, but having cut a road for ten miles from the coast to the interior, we passed over it under the guidance of Mr. Walker, and found the land very rich, with the Cahoon palm the prevailing growth.[4] For half a mile back from the coast—perhaps not quite so far—it will be necessary to corduroy in order to make a firm road, but beyond this nothing of the kind will be necessary.

The ten miles of road terminated at a point on the creek where the bank was fifteen feet high at the time, though the creek was very low—yet there can be no doubt of its being navigable at certain seasons of the year for the "Dorey." We found in our walk a Caoutchouc or India rubber tree that measured twenty inches in diameter and fifty feet to the first limb. A cut with the Machete caused the sap to flow very freely, and to thicken almost instantly under the action of the atmosphere—a portion of which we scraped off, wrapped in a leaf, and placed among the curiosities in our ever present satchel. The sap, when it exudes from the tree is a light cream color, and the quantity that can be obtained from a tree is almost incredible; the flow being much more rapid than we have ever seen from any other tree.

At the landing we found a bamboo that was used as a clothes line, that measured forty-eight feet in length, five inches in diameter at the butt, and two inches in diameter at the other end where it had been cut off, and originally must have been at least sixty feet in length. We also saw an enclosure made with the Pimente, a species of palm growing from twelve to fifteen feet in height and three to four inches in diameter, very straight and without limbs. The fence is made in the following manner: The poles are cut six feet in length, driven into the ground four or six inches, close together, and poles of the same material are placed horizontally within a foot of the top on each side, and opposite, they are then tied with vines, and it is finished.

This material is used very extensively throughout the country, for many purposes. Here we also saw some of the native weather-boarding, made from the cabbage or Royal palm tree. This tree has a very straight, smooth body, frequently being fifty feet high, and a foot in diameter. For half an inch of its depth the wood is solid, but the interior is pithy and not unlike the sugar cane in appearance. This tree is felled, and the exterior of the trunk removed in slabs from ten to fourteen feet in length and four to six inches in width. In using it for weather-boarding, one precaution only is necessary—be careful you do not delay the nail driving, for while you can by the use of a Machete bring down a tree a foot in diameter with a few

4. The author's continuing interest in the presence of the Cahoon palm is due to its being "received as a sure indication of rich land." He notes this in Appendix B on British Honduras.

blows, after these boards become dry they are only fit for the wood pile, as they are as hard as horn. The natives will get out these boards for ten dollars per 1000 superficial feet, and furnish their own provision.

After enjoying the hospitality of Mr. C. and family during the day, we had a discourse from the Rev. Mr. Pearce and at a late hour in the afternoon again boarded our watercraft, and at 6.15 weighed anchor and set sail for "Seven Hills." We had another rain at mid-night, but the deck is our place, as it is decidedly the most comfortable, rain or shine. The cabin and the hold are now decidedly uncomfortable, for two reasons—the want of breeze, and the absence of pure air; those who have taken up their quarters below, finding it necessary to make frequent and often very lengthy visits to the deck in consequences of the character of the vessels' last cargo. Thermometer 6 A.M., 80; 12 M., 82; 6 P.M., 81.

JANUARY 13—At 11 A.M., being opposite the mouth of the Rio Grande, 80 miles from Belize, and six miles from shore, in a perfect calm, Dr. G. A. Frierson and myself took the vessel "Dorey" and two boys of the crew to go ashore for the purpose of getting guides and pitpans of Mr. Bennett, manager of the Seven Hills sugar Estate of Messrs. Young Toledo & Co., to whom our party brought letters from the firm at Belize for the purpose. We landed on an island near the mouth of the river, after having paddled apparently over twice the distance it at first seemed we had to go, and though we found a large native house here, several smaller ones, and three Pitpans, thirty feet in length, concluded to await the arrival of a sail boat three miles north-east of us, and which we hope is coming to the river, before acting farther. Between the schooner and the shore we crossed a shoal that was very thickly strewn with the conch and star-fish, and made several attempts to obtain some with our paddles, but failed to do so—though the water was only five feet deep. The water on the bar at the mouth of the river we found to be four and a half feet deep, the river half a mile from its mouth being from seventy-five to one hundred yards wide. Soon after reaching the island, a fine breeze sprang up from the north-east, which makes it very pleasant sitting under the cocoa nut trees and indulging in the pleasing reflection that we will not be under the necessity of paddling a second time over this waste of water, as our vessel can not fail to be wafted toward us. We found on the island an almond tree sixteen inches in diameter but little fruit on it. The sail boat having passed us, we continued to paddle to a village a few miles off, and proceeded but a short distance when the boys expressed a desire to return to the schooner, as she was heading for the north-east, and we were going from her. We gratified them, and it proved fortunate for us, reaching the vessel at 2:30, over a pretty rough sea for our little craft. A native reached the schooner at the same time, who was on his way to Seven Hill Creek, on which Mr. Bennett lives. From this man it was ascertained we were too far south by eight miles.

While returning to the vessel we saw a Chicken hawk, kingfisher and snipe, which reminded us of—not home—but the land we left. As we paddled along the coast, before returning to the vessel, numbers of a variety of the sardine, of a beautiful purple and gold color, leaped into the boat. After the scales were scraped from them, they were so near transparent that print could be read though [*sic*] their bodies, though they were more than one-fourth of an inch in thickness. They cooked on the schooner, to-day, a cabbage from the cabbage tree, boiling it with bacon as seasoning, and which was found to be very much like the stalk of cabbage of our gardens, though more tender, yet like all substitutes was very far from the original. This cabbage is nothing more than the pith of the top of the trunk of the Royal palm, and may be obtained four inches in diameter and twelve or fifteen inches in length from a tree that is twenty feet high. Reaching the mouth of "Seven Mile" creek, Mr. Morris, Dr. G. A. Frierson and myself proceeded up the creek to the residence of Mr. Bennett, to whom we delivered our letters, and he promised to have at the mouth of the Moho River, 20 miles below Seven Mile creek, for our use, at day-light in the morning, two Dories, properly manned and with competent guides. Soon after we left the vessel a squall came on, with rain, but soon passed off. We were in it long enough to get wet, but are becoming accustomed to that occurrence in this latitude. Here we made our first inquiry concerning the cultivation, or rather growth of corn, yield, etc. Mr. B. stated that he had raised two crops of corn and two crops of rice in one year. (See article on Cereals [in Appendix A, British Honduras].) This place was opened in 1866, the first cutting being done on the 19th of March of that year, and two hundred and fifty acres are now in cultivation, or rather planted in cane; cultivation is no word in this country. We returned to the vessel after dark, and after reporting progress, it was agreed that the party should be divided; one to take a boat and explore the Middle River and Golden Stream, and the other the Moho and Rio Grande. The party to explore the first two rivers, near which we were then anchored, to start in the morning with one of the boats, the other to go on with the schooner to the Rio Grande, where they would be left for the expedition up that river, and the schooner to proceed to the "Moho," still further south, and anchor till all parties should meet again at that place. The party to go above and explore the Golden Stream and Moho rivers to consist of Rev. Mr. Pearce, Mr. Morris, Dr. G. A. Frierson and myself. Mr. Kane went ashore to inform Mr. Bennett of the change in our programme, and we gradually turned to our boards and blankets for the night. Thermometer 6 A.M., 79; 12 M., 82; 6 P.M., 81.

JANUARY 14th—Though we had a heavy rain last night, there is fair prospect of a good day for our expedition, and by 7 A.M. we were on our way for Middle River, which we found to have 3 1–2 feet water at the bar, with mud bottom, into which the pole would sink very readily to a depth of two feet, which is favorable to navigation, all knowing the difference between grounding on mud and on sand. The river is one hundred yards wide at a distance of one hundred and fifty yards from its mouth, and for a distance of two miles is skirted with Mangrove to the water's edge, which growth is somewhat on the Banyan order, its limbs turning to the water and penetrating the mud at the bottom. The Mangrove for the distance mentioned is small, being not more than eight or ten feet high, but after passing the distance named it increases in size to eight inches in diameter and thirty feet in height. The Mangrove is a certain evidence of swampy land, though not always found on low ground. For several miles up this river the land is reserved by Messrs. Toledo & Co., which information we received from one of our party who knew Mr. Bennett, and had been so informed by that gentleman. We found at the distance of three miles from the bar, timber growing to the waters edge, and but little Mangrove. We reached Swazey's landing, which is situated five miles from the bar and on the north bank of the river—at 8:30 A.M. The bank at this place is three feet high, but at a distance of one hundred and forty yards back rises to an elevation of twelve or fourteen feet. This seems to have been selected by Mr. S. as a site for his house, on account of its elevation, he being engaged in cutting Mahogany, but being about through, we were informed he would leave for another locality in a few weeks. Here was seen the first hive of stingless bees. They are about one third smaller than our bees, and producing a very fair quantity of honey, for workmen of their size, would be desirable in any locality where they would live. The hive is a hollow log plugged at each end with wood, and of convenient length for hanging against the side of the house by means of vines. When it is desired to take honey, it is done by removing one of the plugs and breaking the cells containing the honey, by repeated punching with a sharpened stick, when the opposite end is elevated and the honey runs out. The hive we saw was four feet long, and had a hollow about six inches in diameter, and is said to yield in February, at which time it is opened, from two to three quarts of honey, by the means stated. After remaining here a few minutes we moved forward. Three-fourths of a mile above Swazey's the north bank rises to four feet, the surface being covered with coarse grass, while the opposite bank is only two feet high. One fourth a mile further on the bank is not more than fifteen or eighteen inches high, the growth being Cahoon and Pimente. Here the river narrows to twenty yards, with an occasional slough coming to it. We passed a tree fallen into the water, on a limb of which we saw drift four feet above the surface of the water, which clearly indicates the stream is not always as low as at present. The place selected by Dr. F. G. Pew, of Arkansas, was reached at 8.30, the Doctor being found busy with his buildings and clearing. The bank at this point is six feet high, and though the stream is eight yards wide we are at the head of even Dorey navigation; the bottom of the stream is rocky with several large rocks cropping out on either bank. From here, north, the guide informed us, the distance is twelve miles to the Gold-stream. Concluding to go a short distance into the country, we crossed the stream at 10.15 and examined the land for a mile and a half, and returned to our boat thoroughly saturated with water, a very heavy rain having fallen during our trip, from which we had no means of protection.

The ground was very sloppy, and we had some wading to do, though we crossed but one bayou, which will prove an advantage to the ground as a natural drain. Our boatmen, three in number, were as wet as ourselves, but more provident, as they never undertake such expeditions without a "Patikee" in which to carry a change of clothing, and any articles of convenience they may need. The Patikee is a basket made of the splits of a vine called centretie, and in the form of a trunk; the basket sloping upward, in order that the top may fit tightly. These two are covered with palm leaves, and another basket is woven over each, when it is ready for use; not a drop of rain being able to penetrate it.

Bidding adieu to the Doctor at 3 P.M., we moved down the river with the intention of camping near its mouth till morning, when we expect to ascend the Golden-stream. On our way down, seeing a piece of ground about 2 1-2 miles above the mouth that was evidently higher than the surrounding country, and not knowing its extent, we waded across the intervening Mangrove swamp, made an examination and found it to be small in extent, with a large lagoon bounding it on two sides. At 5.05 our boat landed at a small village, half a mile below the river's mouth, where we remained for the night. After cooking and disposing of our simple meal, and enjoying a cup of tea, furnished by the providence of Mr. Morris, we built a fire and engaged in the drying process, which occupied the night to a late hour. The first was made of dry Mahogany, and we can testify to its being most excellent fuel, and the only thing that prevented our having a broil was the want of steak, beautiful coals being on hand in large quantity. The native closed his house at dark in order to keep out musquitoes, all that were in the house having been driven out by the smoke. Mr. P and Dr. F. slung their hammocks, Mr. M. and myself preferring the floor. We slept on a mahogany door, placed without hesitation on the vulgar dirt for our accommodation. Thermometer 6 A.M. 79: 12 M. 78: 6 P.M. 79.

JANUARY 15th—Left camp this morning for the Golden-stream, finding four feet water on the bar, with mud bottom. For a distance of four miles the shore is very low and covered with mangrove, after which timber comes to the waters edge and Pimento is very thick. There is also more or less Mangrove which here grows to forty and fifty feet in height and a foot in diameter—would have taken it for something else, but for the opinion of the guide. At the distance of six miles from the bar, came to a boom placed across the river to catch Mahogany logs, which was crossed without difficulty. Seven miles from the mouth of the river there is three feet bank, with cahoon in abundance, the stream being forty yards wide, with twelve feet water. Half a mile further on we came to another boom, with several hundred Mahogany logs, some of them being three feet in diameter and fifty feet in length; which was crossed after very considerable effort and we again moved forward. Antonio (our guide) informed us that he worked at this point for three years, and that as we ascend the river the land will be found higher. Half a mile further up we were at another boom, larger than the one just crossed and so jammed that no opening could be made without great exertion, and would occupy the entire day. Not feeling disposed to be stopped by such obstacles, it was suggested to Antonio that we make the attempt to cross, which he did not oppose, we having found him at all times very accommodating, but being informed of another boom a short distance above this concluded to go ashore and examine the country, though we were very anxious to go higher. Landing at 12.15 P.M., we followed the course of the river through water and swamp for the distance of a mile and a half, frequently wading to our knees, when we came to the boom we were told of, which rendered it almost unnecessary to cross the one where the boat was secured. The river is here forty yards wide, with plenty of water, and distance from the bay nine miles. The bank is three feet high at this point, and gradually rises till at a distance of thirty yards from the water's edge, it is about ten feet high. From this place we moved in the direction of Swazey's landing (southward) for a distance of one and a half miles, and found a very good country, covered with Cahoon and an undergrowth, not dense, about the size of hoop poles. Coming to a creek which we found to be deep, and not being able to ford it, returned to the boat and at 2.45 again turned our faces toward the "briny deep," reaching the camp of last night at 5.15. Requesting Antonio to make all things ready for our departure at once for the mouth of the Moho, where we expected to find the schooner, he at once proceeded to do so, and at 6 with sails hoisted, though very little breeze, we were on our way and reached the schooner soon after mid-night. On our way down, and when about half an hour out, Antonio boarded the schooner Zenobia, bound for Seven Hills, and the property of Young, Toledo & Co.; he obtained a bottle of Anisett, which caused the blood of the entire party to flow less sluggishly, and brought from "Herado" and "Simon," two of the crew, several Spanish songs, which, together with our sail down the coast with a very gentle and steady breeze, and the rippling of the water as we passed through it, made the trip one of the most pleasant we will probably make during our stay in the country. Most of the party left on the schooner when we departed for Middle river, had gone up the Moho, and we concluded to camp on shore, and follow them after breakfast in the morning. Thermometer, 6 A.M., 80 1-2: 12 M. 82: 6 P.M. 80.

JANUARY 16th—At 8.25 we left for the Moho, finding ------feet water on the bar, and the width of the stream two hundred yards from the mouth, to be one hundred and fifty yards, which is preserved for three fourths of a mile. The south bank, for the distance of a mile is skirted with Mangrove which is larger than that found on either the Middle river or Golden-Stream; the same growth being on the north bank, though smaller.

Three fourths of a mile from the bar a small stream one and a half miles in length, which the natives call "Amargo," enters the river. At the distance of one mile from the bar, timber comes to the waters edge on either side. We tried the temperature of the water and found it to be 76 deg., while the atmosphere was 79 deg. The water is clear and very palatable. One and a half miles from the bar, timber occasionally recedes from the bank for a distance of several yards, the intervening space being covered with Mangrove, which continues for a mile, when timber takes almost entire possession. Not till we had passed over a distance of three and a half miles, did we find Cahoon, and then only one occasionally. At 12 M. we reached the camp of Capt. J. E. Smith, Civil Engineer, who has a number of assistants and is engaged in surveying land for Messrs. Young, Toledo & Co., of Belize. This camp is six feet above the level of the river but the ground recedes. A short distance below here we landed to examine a native's plantation, containing six or eight acres, where we found growing the Pine-apple, sugarcane, cassava, yam and Indian-corn; the owner being in the employ of Mr. Swazey and living on Middle river, many miles distant. The river at Camp Dwight, Capt. Smith's present locality, is sixty yards wide and no bottom with a 20 foot line. Rock was occasionally seen jutting from the bank as we paddled along, though none was visible on the surface of the ground. A heavy rain kept us here till 1.25, when we again pushed out with the hope of overtaking Col. Harrison, who preceded us, having left the vessel yesterday morning, and Camp Dwight at 6 A.M. to-day. Previous to to-day we have been surprised at the scarcity of animal life, so much so that the reader will remember our having mentioned seeing several birds, known to us in the States, but a short distance from Camp Dwight we saw the Iguana in immense numbers, and many birds of beautiful plumage which were unknown to us.

Dr. Frierson shot an Iguana that measured nearly four feet in length, the body being about three inches [?] in diameter at its largest part. For the distance of four miles above Camp Dwight the river is fringed to the water's edge with bamboo, and has an average width of fifty yards. Meeting Col. Harrison, we returned with him, reaching the schooner at 6.20, where the Colonel gave us the following account of his trip. "Found five feet water at the bar, crossed first rapids sixteen miles up, and the second twenty miles from bar, finding two and a half feet water on them and a fall of three feet in one hundred yards; the rapids extending for several hundred yards, no attempt was made to cross them. Here the party landed, and after going two and a half miles north, came to a bayou twelve feet wide with six feet bank, but land flat and wet. Cahoon was found one mile from bank of river. Several gentlemen went south to the base of a mountain or large hill which was found to be less than a mile from the river." Col. H., when we met him on his return, was in company with several boats containing persons engaged in the same undertaking as ourselves, and whom we did not know, none of whom expressed themselves satisfied with what they had seen. Most of these persons had their camp at Ponto-Gordo, a few miles north of the Moho and on the coast. The expedition up the Rio-Grande was made by Capt. Buckner, Mr. Peak and Mr. Owen. From the Captain we received the following report. "Left the schooner soon after you did, entering the river at 9 A.M., and finding it one hundred and fifty yards wide, one hundred and fifty yards from the mouth, which width it retains for half a mile, where it diminishes to one hundred yards; mangrove growing on either side. One and a half miles up, timber reaches the water's edge on the north side, where the bank was found to be five feet high, which continued about the same height as far as 'Big-Hills,' which are ten miles from the bar. There are two other above this, the first being half a mile distant and the other one mile; at the base of which is an old Spanish settlement, with Cocoa nut and Banana trees growing. (Why was this place abandoned?) These hills are about as high as the seven hills—say one hundred and fifty to two hundred feet. At a distance of sixteen miles from the bar, came to a camp established by mahogany cutters, where the party landed and entered the bush for half a mile, but not finding the land to be what they desired returned to their boat, where a native informed them they could go as far as the rapids, thirty miles above, but no further. From this place they returned to the schooner. Thermometer 6 A.M. 71: 12 M. 77: 6 P.M. 77 1-2."

JANUARY 17th—At 9 A.M. our anchor was again brought to the surface and we filled away for Livingston, Guatemala, at the mouth of the Dulce river, which flows from Lake Isabel.[5] We saw on this coast the highest land we had seen since leaving Belize; the mountains frequently coming to the sea. Rain continued during most of last night, but we remained on deck, and succeeded in protecting ourselves pretty well by means of an India rubber coat and umbrella, and in a setting position, slept soundly, as we had often done before. At noon we tried a stewed Iguana, prepared in the most approved style by the schooner's cook, and after laying aside all prejudice, it was pronounced equal to young squirrel in delicacy of flavor.

To-day was showery and disagreeable in the extreme. A squall struck us at 1.20 P.M., which made the little vessel enter the harbor of Livingston with great speed, and we came to anchor at 1.40. At the time of our leaving Belize there was some cholera reported at the place, which was not unknown at Livingston. Soon as we anchored a health officer came aboard, and we were informed it was necessary for us to go into quarantine, for several days, before we could come on shore. This was a disappointment, as we desired to visit Lake Isabel, and to ramble over a little high ground, but could not think of subjecting ourselves to the modest requirement of several days quarantine. Not being able to go ashore we succeeded in replenishing our stock of fluids with several bottles of native rum, though the person who brought it out could not tread the deck of the vessel. Presume the health

5. The 1830s was a decade of intense Liberal reform in Guatemala and included adopting the so-called Livingston judicial codes, which Edward Livingston had drawn up in 1824 for Louisiana. The codes included equality before the law, trial by juries of peers, and an enlightened (and expensive) system of incarceration and rehabilitation for convicted criminals. They were too progressive for the Louisiana legislature, which rejected them. Guatemalan Liberals were so profoundly impressed by Livingston, who became secretary of state in Andrew Jackson's administration, that they named the Caribbean port after him. Mario Rodriguez, *A Palmerstonian Diplomat in Central America: Frederick Chatfield, Esq.* (Tucson: University of Arizona Press, 1964).

officer thought he was perfectly safe along side—we sincerely hope he is still living.

As this section of the world is said to be infested with snakes, and alcoholic liquor being considered in our land a specific for their bite, on the principle of alcohol not being digested, but passing off through the circulation, and one poison neutralizing another, we can confidently recommend the rum of Livingston for the purpose named, as we certainly never tested such villainous stuff before, during the whole course of our lives, not excepting the *Pine top* of Confederate times which it leaves in the shade as completely as the "God of day" does the refulgent beams of a farthing rush light. Thanks, however, to the gentleman who was kind enough to obtain it for us, it was undoubtedly the best he could do. We also obtained of Mr. --- a bunch of fine fish which were the first since leaving Belize; having failed in all our efforts to catch any by trolling as we sailed along the coast. Livingston seemed to be a very small place, we saw only a few houses, near the bluff, on which it is situated, and which is from twenty to thirty feet in height. At 4 o'clock, the stiff breeze from the north-west that prevailed at the time we cast anchor having subsided, we moved away from Livingston in the direction of Omoa, in the Republic of Honduras. Thermometer, 6 A.M. 72; 12 M. 75; 6 P.M. 74.

JANUARY 18th.—A heavy rain this morning at an unseasonable hour stirred up the deck sleepers, and the water was so rough that several of the party were sea-sick. As we sailed along, the coast presents the same appearance as at and near Livingston, the mountains coming to the sea. We ought to have reached Omoa during the night, but did not till a late hour in the afternoon, and while rapidly approaching the harbor the captain was hailed from a small boat, in a language we did not understand, but its magic effect was at once visible, for never did anchor of the same weight reach bottom quicker in the same depth of water than did that of the "Three Sisters," and we were still. Horror of horrors, the authorities are afraid of cholera,—but will see us in the morning. Visions of quarantine rise before us, shutting out from our view all that is beautiful and crowding from the memory all that is hopeful. One thing we felt assured of, if they wanted a cholera germ at Omoa, it would only be necessary to keep us in the Pigsty we were occupying and they would get it of the most virulent type. We determined to go ashore the next day, if not at Omoa, at some other place. For some days past nearly every hygienic law has been transgressed, and for the first time in our life we were inclined to doubt that "Disease is in many cases consequent upon the violation of a law of nature." Thermometer, 6 A.M. 77; 12 M., 78 1-2; 6 P.M. 79.

The Republic of Honduras

JANUARY 19.—We passed a very disagreeable night, having frequent showers, but were cheered by the sun's appearance at 7.30, and we proceeded to "hang out" our clothes, blankets, etc. Having left nearly all our baggage at Belize we frequently find it difficult to raise a dry garment when the rain continues. The celebrated fort of Omoa is within a short distance of us, but the town is half a mile back, and looks rather *small for its age.*

At 8 A.M., Dr. De Soto, the health officer came on board, and finding each individual in possession of a cup of coffee and hard tack concluded we were all right, and returned to report. In an hour and a quarter, seemingly a very long time; permission was granted us to go ashore, of which we were not slow to avail ourselves, and very soon all were once more on *Terra firma.* We "put up" at Belisles' Hotel, and had the best of the season placed before us in the greatest variety and prepared in the most approved styles. Belisle or as he is called by most persons the "judge," is quite a noted individual— holding several offices of a civil character, and is the only hotel keeper in the place. You are not roused from your slumbers by the discordant gong, or the unpleasant bell, but by the dulcet notes of a very large hand organ, which is played with great skill by the judge himself.

We have yet to hear of the first persons going to the Judge hungry and leaving unfed, or going without money and going away empty. We were the recipients of many kindnesses from the Judge, in the case of articles left with him, and in other ways, and on all occasions found him equal to any trust confided to him. We reached shore in time for breakfast, which, according to the custom of the country is placed on the board at 10 A.M., coffee having been served at 7, and which is considered sufficient foundation, but confess we always felt, before the breakfast hour, that our foundation would hardly support the superstructure we were expected to place upon it.

Insertion, pp. 120–121 in original

OMOA

The town of Omoa has less than one thousand inhabitants, and contains no buildings worthy of note, most of the houses being one story, though some are covered with tiles and some with corrugated iron. The system of cleanliness in operation at Belize, is unknown here, and even hogs are slaughtered in the streets.

OMOA, FROM THE LAND.

7. City of Omoa. E. G. Squier, *The States of Central America* (New York: Harper & Brothers, 1858), 108.

Commandant of Omoa . . . . Gen'l Phil. Espinoza.
American Consul . . . . Charles Follin.
Belgian and British Consul . . . . J. F. Debrot
French Consul . . . . St. Laurent.

End of Insertion

At 1 P.M., Col. Harrison and myself obtained horses and under guidance of a gentleman who had visited the coast, made a trip to "Port Cables" [Puerto Caballos, subsequently Puerto Cortés], about ten miles distant, and the northern terminus of the projected interoceanic railroad that is to run from the bay of Farseca [Fonseca] on the south, and which was surveyed by Mr. Trautwine in 1858 at an expense of two hundred thousand dollars. The length of route surveyed being about one hundred and fifty miles. We passed on our route a tree of gigantic size said to be the one under which Cortes gave *"Gracias a Dios"* for his escape from the many perils by which he was beset in his travels. The port is situated at the head of a beautiful bay and had one of the finest harbors in the world; maps prepared in England from coast surveys, show that the largest vessels can anchor within a very short distance of the coast in perfect safety, and small craft can come within one hundred yards of the shore.

Col. McDermott and several others we found at this place, who intend locating near by, but had not, we believe, positively decided where. The colonel seemed very enthusiastic, and we certainly hope he may realize every expectation.[6] At 4.30 we started on our return for Omoa, but in consequence of the character of the road over which we had to pass, much of it being at the beach, and the surf rolling in very heavily, concluded to stop for the night with the magistrate of *Cienagueta*, Mr. Robinson, who placed before us for supper, coffee, wheat bread and *fried Panoti*. We are learning to eat what is placed before us, and seldom ask questions. The Panot we found to appear and taste much like the flesh of the Dorey; the meat on its breast being quite an inch thick, and very tender. We have tried to eat Panot since then, and to place ourselves right and not to appear to occupy a false position, will state that they were invariably so tough that parboiling and hashing were necessary to enable one to think of attempting to digest it.

On the route between Omoa and the port it is necessary to pass through two Carib villages, Cienagueta and Tulian, and to cross the Tulian and Marquez rivers, the first by fording and the second by boat, leaving your horses behind. This river runs from the Marquez Lagoon, immediately in rear of the port, and flows into the sea less than half a mile below. There are also several mountain streams of small size, all of which together with the Tulian, have rapid currents over rocky bottoms and the water very clear, cool and palatable. Thermometer 6 A.M., 76; 12 M., 80; 6 P.M., 77.

JANUARY 20th—At 7 this morning we again made a start for Omoa, stopping on the way to examine a Coffee Estate, or Rancho, which was the first we had seen. (For description see "Productions of Honduras." [Appendix B]) We were informed on this trip that the Chamlicon river could be navigated to within three miles of San Pedro Sula. If it is so, why pass over the mountains? We will make further inquiry on this point. The road for two miles from Omoa was very sloppy, and when we reached town, at 9.10, we looked as though we had just made an extensive trip over a hitherto unexplored Louisiana swamp in the rainy season, and had several times lost our way. Having quite a quantity of clothing that rubbing as well as wetting will improve, several of us repaired to the Omoa river to see what improvement we could make in their appearance. We washed and spread on the rocks, and by the time the last was spread the first were ready for the ironing room. In the afternoon, Dr. Gray, Dr. Ryan, Rev. Mr. Pearce and Mr. Morris engaged a Dorey and started, the first for Lake Isabel, Dr. Ryan

---

6. Sheila Brannon ("Articles about Dermott," 3, www.seark.net/~sabra/der.html) describes the McDermott venture to Honduras "a failure, due to dysentery, the climate and other hardships." There were eight McDermotts on the ship from Belize that docked in New Orleans in December 1868 (Simmons 2001: 129).

for Porto-Gordo, where he left his family, and the Rev. Mr. Pearce and Mr. Morris for Belize, via "Seven Hills."

The rest of us, except Dr. G. P. Frierson and Mr. Daniel Swett, who will remain here, or endeavor to reach San Pedro via the Chamlicon river, hope to get off to-morrow, taking the mule and mountains as our mode of conveyance and route. Col. H., Dr. F., Mr. D.S. and myself paid our respects to-day to the Commandant of Omoa, Genl. Espanoza, by whom we were very kindly received, and who expressed great satisfaction at the prospect of our citizens emigrating to the Republic; making known to us that land could be obtained gratis, and if we should be so fortunate as to find an unclaimed *gold mine*, that the authorities of the nearest municipality would cause to be surveyed a certain distance north, east and west, of the point we should designate, which would establish our claim. It is hardly necessary to say we did not have any surveying done. Thermometer 6 A.M., 72; 12 M., 80 1-2; 6 P.M., 78.

JANUARY 21st.—At 9 o'clock this morning we were mounted and off for the far famed San Pedro Sula, and reached the Rancho Grande, eighteen miles distant, at 3 P.M., where we had the pleasure of meeting Mr. Reynaud, owner of the premises, and Governor of the Circuit of San Pedro; and saw the operation of winnowing coffee to remove the husk, which is done by the ordinary fan mill, which we found on examination to have been made by Allen & Co., of New York. Here we saw coffee in every stage, and were informed by the Governor that he has forty-five hundred bearing trees, producing, he can not say how much, but will know at the close of the season, as he is keeping an accurate account of the crop as gathered. (See Appendix B—productions of Honduras.) The residence at the Rancho is constructed in a very substantial manner, of brick, plastered inside and out, and covered with tiles. The plantation is a bowl, surrounded by mountains, and is said to be twenty-five hundred feet above the level of the sea. The Rio Grande, about forty yards wide, clear and cool from the mountains, flows by a short distance from the house, and is easily forded. To-day has been cloudy with occasional showers, and though the thermometer indicates 77 deg. at 4 o'clock P.M., our feelings are decidedly in favor of fire, which would be very comfortable. Thermometer 6 A.M., 74, 12 M. 74 1-2, 6 P.M. 73 1-2.

JANUARY 22ND.—Left Rancho Grande at 7 this morning, reaching the foot of the mountains on the opposite slope at 9.10, and moved along their base for a distance of fifteen miles through a beautiful avenue formed by the branches of the Cahoon Palm that gracefully curve over the road, in many places entirely shutting out the sun's rays. Stopped at the village of Chiloma, on the Chiloma river, for breakfast at 10.40. We found here the Umbrella China tree growing in perfection, which we never saw in Mississippi, though it is planted in Texas for its shade. At 12.30 P.M. we were again in the saddle, and crossed the Rio Blanco four miles from San Pedro which we found to be forty yards wide, very shallow, sand bottom and water warm and very unpalatable; the Thermometer indicating in the atmosphere 83½ and in the water 89 deg., time 2.30 P.M. Two miles from San Pedro we crossed the Mermijo, fifteen yards wide, and about twelve to eighteen inches deep—the same as the last two crossed—water clear and bottom sandy. Several fields of Corn were passed by us, and a field of Cotton, entirely stripped of foliage. Our journey terminated at 3.20, and we found ourselves in a place where the houses did not prevent our seeing the town. Through the kindness of Mr. Reynaud we were provided with an excellent dinner, to which we did ample justice. Thermom. 6 A.M., 70; 12 M., 79; 6 P.M., 78.

Insertion, pp. 113–114 in original

SAN PEDRO SULA

The town of San Pedro is situated on the plain of Sula, in the department of Santa Barbara, and is about thirty miles from Omoa, though the natives state the distance to be about fifty miles. An *attempt* has been made to describe the routs [*sic*] to it, and we will now give a short account of the town and its surroundings. The town is certainly most delightfully situated, two and a half miles from the mountains on the west, whose tops are frequently enveloped in clouds, and the varying hues of the vegetation on their slopes as the sun rises and descends make a scene that is constantly changing, and which is as pleasing as it is lovely. There are no cisterns or well, the supply of water being brought from the *Rio de las Piedras*, two and a half miles distant, and passes through the place by four little streams, through which it gurgles over pebbly bottoms, entirely shaded till it reaches the corporate limits of the place. Pure, clear and cool from the mountains.

By a regulation of the town the water is not permitted to be disturbed above a certain point, where the supply is obtained for culinary purposes and for drinking. The *Cavildo* (Court house) is constructed of large sun dried bricks, or adobes, and is covered with tiles, as is also the church edifice and several other houses in the place, but most of the buildings have mud walls and are covered with branches of the Cahoon. Not a chimney is to be seen in the place; not a pane of glass; and only two plank floors. The houses are all one story. The country north, south and east of town is cultivated in patches of from five to fifty acres, where the orange, plantain, banana, pine-apple and other fruits may be found growing. From sun rise till noon it is best to keep in the shade as the heat is oppressive, but after that time we have never known a breeze to fail to spring up from the north, which prevails with greater or less force till sunset. It is a somewhat re-markable fact that when the thermometer indicates 70°, the temperature, judging from the feelings, seems to be at least 10° lower. The least that can be said is, this is a lovely spot, but the means of getting to it, and other ob-jections that seem insurmountable, should, if possible, be removed. Popu-lation from 500 to 600; 200 of which are emigrants [immigrants], and the remainder mixed.

Insertion, pp. 87–88 in original

Perhaps Spanish Honduras, particularly San Pedro and vicinity, received attention from our countrymen at as early a day as British Honduras. Major Green Malcolm, of Kentucky, left Atlanta, Georgia, in April 1867, for San Pedro, via Omoa, with seventy souls. Soon after their arrival at San Pedro it was decided to place the government of their local interests under the control of a council, in order to avoid the necessity of assembling the entire colony when any question of interest or expediency should arise likely to ef-fect [*sic*] their welfare, and at a public meeting they elected as their council the following gentlemen: Maj. Malcolm as their presiding officer.

G. Malcolm	Geo. W. Walters
L. G. Pirkle	J. H. Wade
H. H. Briers	P. Goldsmith, Secy.

MEDINA

The site for a town to be called Medina, in honor of the President of the Republic, was selected soon after the arrival of Major Malcolm, but up to the time of our leaving San Pedro it did not contain a finished house, and only three or four were in course of construction. The site selected adjoins the corporation of San Pedro.

The land examined to-day was found to be of every character known to this country, except rock; at times covered with cahoon, and high and dry, with very rich soil; and at other times lower and wet, with the same growth, when it changes to a gravel sub-soil but a few inches below the surface, and at times to portions covered with heavy grass. We have frequently been surprised to find so large an admixture of sand where it was reasonable to expect but little, though the growth even on such land was very heavy, and the cahoon nearly always present in greater or less quantity.

On our return to San Pedro we were much disposed to think the guide, who has made two unsuccessful attempts to convey us to our point of destination, unreliable, and it was determined to employ another, who said he could find the river, if we would furnish him with men to assist in cutting, and pay him if he accomplished his object; if not, no pay. Many lime trees were found today, the fruit being quite as large as the lemons imported into the United States. The natives being thirsty drank from a *water vine*, a piece of which, four feet in length and three inches in diameter yielded a pint of very palatable fluid, devoid of any green or sappy taste, which quenched the thirst very quickly. This morning was showery, and we were alternately wet and dry, though we feel no inconvenience from it. Thermometer 6 A.M., 72 1-2; 12 M., 81; 6 P.M., 73 1-2.

JANUARY 26.—This morning we saw the first fog since leaving Belize. At 12 M., Col. H. and myself, accompanied by Dr. Scott, who has for seven years resided at San Pedro, visited the site of old San Pedro, two miles south-west of the present town of that name, which we found overgrown to such an extent that we saw nothing more than the remains of what we were told was the wall surrounding the place at the time of its destruction. We moved on to where the *Rio de los Piedras* issues from the mountains, and following its course for a mile we crossed a stream known as *Santa Anna*, and at a distance of two miles from here, following the base of the mountains, we came to the *Mermijo*, at the point where it comes from the mountains. All these streams are clear, cool and very rapid, although small. The *San Pedro* and *Rio de los Piedras* unite about four miles from where the latter makes its exit from the mountains, and not far below this the Rio de los Piedras unites with the Mermijo, near where the latter crosses the road from San Pedro to Omoa. Nearly all the country between San Pedro and the mountains, on the west, *has at some time been under cultivation*, but is now covered with undergrowth, except where small clearings have been recently made. Thermometer 6 A.M., 72; 12 M., 81 1-2; 6 P.M., 76.

End of Insertions

JANUARY 23rd—We breakfasted at 11 A.M., though coffee was served at 7, mounted our mules at 12, and accompanied by Maj. G. Malcolm rode around to inspect the country; following the Comayagua road, running south from San Pedro, for half a mile, at which point we left it, moving to the east-crossing the Tipiaca two miles from town and following the same road to the Rio Blanco, four miles from town, beyond which the land is claimed by Mr. Debrot, of Omoa. On our way back we passed a cotton field which we were informed was without leaves three weeks ago, but is now in full foliage, though the genuine *Army worm* is again at work and will soon have it stripped once more. The country over which we passed is very flat, with Cahoon the prevailing growth, though the soil contained a very large proportion of sand. The rivers above named are quite small, being from fifteen to twenty yards wide at the time we visited them, and about two feet deep, with sandy bottoms, though the water was not very clear nor cool, but palatable. We reach San Pedro in time for dinner at 5; the order of our meals will in future be as follows: Coffee at 7, breakfast at 11, dinner at 5. Thermometer 6 A.M., 75; 12 M., 78 1-2; 6 P.M., 78.

JANUARY 24.—At 8.30 this morning we were again on the way to continue our explorations, Maj. M. again accompanying us. Our object to-day being to strike the Tacomiche river immediately below the junction of the Tipiaca and Blanco, which form it. The general direction of these rivers is south-east, and their waters flow to the Chemlicon, the general direction of which is northeast to the Gulf of Honduras. After passing over the road pursued yesterday for two and a half miles, we turned to the south-east, crossing more wet land than we expected to see, and passing over quite a large piece of ground covered with very coarse grass growing from three to four feet high. Our conjectures were that a swamp must be near, and though we had a guide and several men armed with the Machete to cut the way, our fears were soon realized; our horses moving forward with difficulty, which increased till necessity compelled a return. On the way out, the animals we were riding fell, but rose without our dismounting, and despite their exertions, fell again, and being unable to rise we dismounted and waded out, when the course was changed further to the south, which we followed till satisfied we were on a large body of good land when we struck for the Comayagua wood, which was reached two miles from San Pedro.

From this point several of the party returned to town, while Col. H., Capt. B., Dr. F. and myself concluded to visit the Chamlicon river, said to be five miles distant. On our way we crossed the La Puerta, three miles from town, which is a very small stream, and a few hundred yards beyond turned to the left in order to follow the Comayagua road, the other crossing the mountains close by. The river where we struck it is from seventy-five to one hundred yards wide, with two and a half feet of water on the rapids at this point, and has all the characteristics of mountain streams, being clear, cool and drinkable. After enjoying the *luxury* of a bath, we retraced our steps toward San Pedro, meeting our *Chef de cuisine*, whom the Colonel had sent back to obtain refreshments for the inner man. Seating ourselves on the grass a hearty meal was soon made on eggs, corn bread and beef. It may be well to state that this proved to be the first and last time we had corn bread placed before us during our stay in Spanish Honduras, and up to this time have seen no preparation of flour since leaving Omoa.

After our meal, Col. H and myself started for the mountains, two and a half miles east of San Pedro, but the day being far spent with every prospect of rain, returned to our quarters. The distance from San Pedro to the Chamlicon by the Comayagua road is seven miles; three miles of the way being almost entirely level, and could with little labor be made an excellent carriage road. Beyond the "Puerta" the road is very rocky for most of the way to the river. The land seen to-day is generally better than that seen yesterday, covered with cahoon and having several natural drains running through it. At the Puerta musquitoes annoyed us very much, though we were not troubled by them yesterday nor to-day up to this time. We have found bars unnecessary to our comfort at San Pedro, not having seen, felt or heard a musquito at that place. Thermometer 6 A.M. 73 1-2; 12 M. 82; 6 P.M. 78.

JANUARY 25.—Our attempt to reach the Tacomiche yesterday proving unsuccessful, though it is reported to be only five miles from San Pedro, we were again in the saddle this morning at 8, to try another route, which we did by keeping a general course to the southeast from San Pedro till we reached what the natives call the Tipiaca mountain, about five miles from San Pedro, and no river being in sight we deemed it best to return and adopt some more certain method of accomplishing our object. On our way this morning we passed an old plantation of 62 Cocoa trees quite full of fruit. Over a considerable portion of our route to-day the country presented the appearance of once having been in cultivation, and on making enquiry concerning it, we received the assurance that such was the fact. Why was the cultivation of this section discontinued by those who burnt the bush and ate the produce of the soil perhaps a century ago?

JANUARY 27.—This morning, at 8.40, Messrs. Kane, Owen, Peak and Dr. G. A. Frierson left us on their return to Omoa, the first two intending to extend their trip to the United States, but soon to return, and the others to proceed to Belize for baggage left there by the entire party.

William, our *chef de cuisine*, accompanied Mr. Owen to Louisiana, but expressed his determination to return, and thought he would be able to bring others with him. Dr. F. and Mr. D.S. not having made their appearance, we have written to them to make the attempt via the Zequisiesta, which empties in to the Chemblicon, and is stated to be navigable for Dories to within fourteen and a half miles of San Pedro, whither we will send mules for them as soon as we hear of their having left Omoa; the road being represented to be good. We will take a rest to-day, and hope to-morrow to be able to visit the *Zacomiche*. Thermometer 9 A.M., 69; 12 M., 78 1-2; 6 P.M., 77.

JANUARY 28.—At 8.20 this morning our entire party was again in the saddle, Maj. Malcolm accompanying us, and we were off for the Zacomiche, which was *discovered* yesterday, crossing the *Tipiaca* two miles east of town, and taking a course east by south, we reached the river at 12.10, about seven miles from San Pedro, and found it to be eight yards wide and three and a half feet deep. This is the river we were told would be navigated by a *steamer* to be brought out on the next trip of the Tradewind. Most of the land passed over was found to be much the same as that already described. At the water's edge we found musquitoes, but none as we approached the river, and as singular as it may appear, we took a nap within twenty yards of the water and were unmolested by them. Several Iguanas were seen to-day, the first we have found since leaving the Moho in British Honduras. Most of the party engaged in fishing catching several cats and one of a kind known to the natives as "Sleeping-fish," which was very much like the cat in appearance, but having scales.

Captain Buckner took the guide with him and endeavored to reach the mouth of the river, which was supposed to be close by, but after going three miles, without success, gave it up and we all returned to San Pedro as soon as he rejoined us. Thermometer 6 A.M. 67: 12 M. 85: 6 P.M. 81: 9 P.M., 75.

JANUARY 29th.—This morning we accompanied Maj. Malcolm to his kitchen garden, where kale, mustard, turnips, tomatoes, snap-beans, okra, pumpkins and black-eyed peas, were found growing and looking well. His cotton field was also visited, and plenty of eggs found to produce another supply of worms, and but a few days can elapse before they will be at work, and the destruction of foliage is but a question of time, and a very short time at that; notwithstanding, Maj. Malcolm and many whose fields have been stripped, still think they will make half a crop. Thermometer 6 A.M. 71; 9 A.M. 81; 12 M 86; 3 P.M. 88; 6 P.M. 80; 9 P.M. 78.

JANUARY 30.—To-day being showery and very disagreeable, we kept within doors. In the evening, though the Thermometer indicated 70 deg., we made a fire and sat near it with great comfort. Thermometer 6 A.M. 71 deg. 9 A.M. 72 deg., 12 M. 72 deg. 6 P.M. 70 deg. 9 P.M. 67 1-2 deg.

JANUARY 31st.—The bad weather continuing, we made a feeble effort at visiting on a small scale, but most of the time kept our room, as rain fell at intervals during the entire day. Thermometer 6 A.M. 64; 9 A.M. 65 1-2; 12 M. 69 1-2; 3 P.M. 70; 6 P.M. 72 1-2; 9 P.M. 70.

FEBRUARY 1st.—No rain this morning, though the atmosphere is damp and chilly and to such an extent that our fire is kept up, and with the party around, it reminds us of camp. We saw to-day Irish potatoes, grown here from seed brought from the States, which were of respectable size, but are said to be inclined to be watery, though the sweet potato does well, according to report. By invitation we visited the field of Mr. -----Jack, where the sarsaparilla was seen growing, though none had up to this time been gathered. Though there was some prospect at an early hour this morning of a fair day, we have had repeated showers. Thermometer 6 A.M. 65; 9 A.M. 68; 12 M. 70 1-2; 3 P.M. 71 1-2; 9 P.M. 70.

FEBRUARY 2nd.—A courier was sent to the gentlemen who remained behind when we left Omoa, several days since; he should be back to-day, and his failure to appear will necessitate a trip to that place, to carry out the object for which he was sent. To our great astonishment, Mr. D. S., and Dr. F., and two sons made their appearance this afternoon, having crossed the mountains, on mules. As one of the riders weighs two hundred and forty pounds, he can best tell how the trip was made, though the mule would undoubtedly have something to say if endowed with the power of speech, for his weight did not greatly exceed the burden he had to carry. These gentlemen left Omoa on last Wednesday, 29th ult., but were detained at the Rancho by bad weather till this morning. Thermometer 6 A.M. 68 1-2; 9 A.M. 69; 12 M. 72; 3 P.M. 74; 6 P.M. 72; 9 P.M. 71.

FEBRUARY 3rd.—A Dorey said to be drawing two feet, arrived this morning at the village of Chemlicon, on the river of the same name, within seven miles of San Pedro, loaded with freight from Cienagueta. We were told nine days were required to make the trip; our efforts to obtain the particulars of the trip were, however, entirely unsuccessful. Colonel H., Dr. F., and Mr. D.S., accompanied by Dr. Scott, who kindly offered his services as guide, made a trip to the mountains west of San Pedro, returning late in the evening drenched by rain which fell heavily during the day.

This may not be the "rainy season," but it is certainly a season of rain. Thermometer 6 A.M. 68 1-2; 9 A.M. 72; 12 M. 75; 3 P.M. 72; 6 P.M. 77 1-2.

FEBRUARY 4th.—Our party explored the country to-day between San Pedro and the mountains west, finding some excellent land between the Los Piedras and Mermijo, though on the latter, and for some distance from its right bank it was found to be very sandy. This exploration was made on foot, with compass in hand, and though we had two natives to use the machete found the trip very fatiguing and will not soon be caught making a similar one.

We returned to San Pedro at a late hour, but the bath and change of clothing could not be deferred, for we are well acquainted with the Agarra-pata. This is a very good place to describe this pest. It is nothing more than the small wood tick, called by some "seed-tick." They are so small as almost to require a magnifying glass to make them visible, and figures would fail to make their number known. Any one going to the woods is certain to return with thousands of them. We always adopted every precaution against them, such as tying the pants close around the ancle [*sic*] and brushing off repeatedly with a bunch of twigs. We have seen the most fearful effects produced by them where these precautions were neglected. It is said they are not troublesome for more than two months in the year, but we were unable to ascertain what two months. Perhaps the sixty days you are supposed to be *absent* from the place were referred to. Thermometer 6 A.M. 68; 12 M. 75; 6 P.M. 78.

FEBRUARY 5th.—Colonel H., Captain B. and myself endeavored to ascend the mountains to-day in order to get a view of that portion of the valley of Sula, in which San Pedro is situated; our horses were used as far as possible, when we dismounted and began the ascent, walking till tired, resting and again pushing on, which was repeated, though we did not succeed in reaching the top. An elevation was attained, however, that gave us a magnificent view of the valley below, seemingly stretching to the east for twenty miles and to the south to nearly double that distance. But for the rain and clouds we would have had a better view, but we were amply repaid for our toil. Mr. D.S. had a chill to-day, which is pretty good evidence this latitude can produce the "Bilious Intermittent." Thermometer 6 A.M. 74; 12 M. 78; 6 P.M. 76.

FEBRUARY 6th.—We are still unable to exclaim, "Behold how brightly breaks the morn," for rain is again falling, and the heavens are entirely overcast. The rain continued during the day with a short intermission at noon. Thermometer 6 A.M. 74; 12 M 82; 6 P.M. 76.

FEBRUARY 7th.—A miserable day was this to the writer, as the "Bilious Intermittent" culminated and he shivered. Perhaps he did not wish he was home! His bed was a blanket spread on not a large quantity of shavings, which had a dirt floor foundation. Why didn't he go to the Hotel? Hotel! Let us drop this subject. Mr. D.S. is now quite well, but when sick it required the united efforts of two individuals for forty-eight hours to secure a hide bottomed bedstead, for which it was agreed seventy-five cents per month should be paid. Thermometer 6 A.M. 69.

FEBRUARY 8th.—Rain again to-day. Having heard of several persons being down with chills, we are naturally led to inquire into the cause. Is it the rain, change of weather, heat, fatigue, or is it the result of malarious influences? Being unable to say, we can only testify to the complaint being, if not the most dangerous, the most disagreeable disease known to the human family, and persons here not unfrequently have them of the quotidian type for a week at a time. All emigrants are requested by Gov. Reynaud to meet at the *Cavildo* (Court-house) tomorrow morning, to hear read a translation of the concessions made by the Puebla (town) of San Pedro Sula, for their benefit. Information has reached here of the arrival of sixty-four persons at Omoa, destined for this place, and quite a large number being at Belize, also coming here.

FEBRUARY 9th.—Notwithstanding we should look for a chill to-day, visited the Cavildo, remaining but a short time, as we have not only heard the concessions read, but have a copy in the original, in our possession.

FEBRUARY 10th.—Thermometer 6 A.M. 67 1-2 deg. 12 M. 83 deg. 6 P.M. 77 1-2 deg.

FEBRUARY 11th.—Thermometer 6 A.M. 67 1-2 deg. 12 M. 83 deg. 6 P.M. 77 1-2 deg.

FEBRUARY 12th.—Having kept quiet during the past two days, and no repetition of our chill, feel pretty safe for the present. All complained of having slept cold last night notwithstanding blankets and closed doors. Information was received this morning of Mr. Peak and Dr. Frierson, who have arrived at Omoa with the baggage and supplies of the party, will come forward via the Chemlicon and Tequisiesta as soon as they can make arrangements for so doing. It is their intention to bring the freight to a point within fourteen miles of San Pedro, from which it will be brought here by wagon, there being two of those very convenient vehicles for the conveyance of goods at this place, and plenty of oxen. Thermometer 6 A.M. 64 1-2; 12 M. 79; 6 P.M. 70.

FEBRUARY 13th.—To-day information was received that Mr. P. and Dr. F., left Omoa several days since and ascended the Chemlicon to the Tequisiesta, when, in consequence of low water and obstructions in the river, they returned to the bar at the mouth of the Chemlicon, there to remain until instructions should be received from here. All were much disappointed at this delay, as they have been without their Sunday clothes for nearly six weeks. Thermometer 6 A.M. 74; 12 M. 80 1-2; 6 P.M. 76.

FEBRUARY 14th.—It was decided this morning that Captain Buckner and myself should take a Dorey and men at the ford of the Chemlicon, seven miles south-east of here and proceed to the bar of the river and assist the gentlemen in charge of the baggage, they having had a serious time of it since leaving Omoa. Our preparations were hastily made, and consisted of blanket, bar, mackintosh, india-rubber coat and jerked beef; our dependence for bread being the plantain, a quantity of which we intended taking with us from the crossing, and to replenish our stock as needed at the various plantations we expected to pass. The Captain and myself left San Pedro at 10 A.M., and at 11.30 reached the village of Chemlicon, and presented the letter kindly furnished by Gov. Reynaud, and which expressed the desire that we should be furnished with two men and a Dorey for the trip. Our main dependence was a man named John, who it was ascertained after considerable delay, was in San Pedro, consequently we must await his return. On our way back to recross the river we visited a hot sulphur spring, not more than thirty yards from the river's bank, the temperature of which we could not ascertain, having left our thermometer at San Pedro, but it was evidently very high, steam being distinctly visible even at noon-day as the water bubbled up. We will endeavor to visit this spot again, and get a bottle of water for analysis. When we recrossed the river, John was on hand, but of course could not think of making a start till morning, this being the natives' peculiar habit in all such cases, and having sent our horses back, will remain here till morning, at which time there is fair prospect of our getting an early start. Thermometer 6 A.M. 73; 12 M. 76; 6 P.M. 78.

FEBRUARY 15.—At 6:30 we were off, and although we expected to have John only, or two men at most, find a boy in the boat whose duty will be to use a pole. At 7.40 a point was passed known to the natives as Juarlomo, though nothing was in sight save a girl washing clothes; and at 8.15 an island, and at 8.30 another neither of which contained more than three or four acres; and at 8.45 another, about 10 acres in extent, the growth on which is principally willow. The mouth of the *Tacomiche* was passed at 11 and the Cow pen reached at 11:30, (This point is known as the Cow Pen, because it was used in years past as a place for assembling cattle for the use of Mahogany cutters.) Nearly opposite this place one of the boatmen owns a plantation and the boat was stopped there in order that a supply of plantains might be laid in for the voyage. The Cow pen is situated at the base of quite a large hill, and the bank is from eight to ten feet high. We pushed out at 12 M., and at 2 passed a piece of ground on our right that had the appearance of an immense clearing, covered with high grass, and hardly a tree on it, and appeared to contain several hundred acres. The same character of country was seen a few miles below, but the patches did not seem so extensive. John informed us that though this ground is covered with grass, and peat, it is not swampy. Want of time prevented our making such an examination as we desired, but at 2.45 we went ashore to examine, by climbing a tree, this peculiar and not uninteresting country, and to ascertain to what extent a kind of willow existed that was occasionally seen. Over thousands of acres the grass extends with here and there an isolated willow, the bank at the waters edge being four feet high. Was this district of country cleared by man; and if so, why is it not now made to produce something for his support? For several miles we passed through country that presented much the same appearance, the grass being on either shore—the bank three feet high and river fifty yards wide. At 3 P.M. we left the main river and entered a "cut off" at our right. (This cut off was made by a raft in the river a mile or two below, which entirely prevents navigation by the main stream,) we passed over a foot fall in entering the "cut off" which at this place is ten yards wide eight feet deep, and has a current of about *seven miles* an hour.

The utmost skill was necessary on the part of the boatmen to avoid running into the bank and against fallen trees, or sunken logs, and to prevent our being dragged into the water by over-hanging limbs. At 3 P.M., a piece of low marshy ground was reached, and an occasional Mangrove seen—depth of water four feet. As good camping ground is not easily found, availed ourselves of the first that offered and at 5 stopped for the night. Thermometer, 6 A.M. 71: 12 M. 72: 6 P.M. 73.

FEBRUARY 16th—Left camp this morning at 6.30. The stream here is about twenty yards wide, but as we advanced, would at times become narrow, and in the course of the morning we passed over portions not more than four yards wide, and over several miles that did not exceed six in width, and a current varying from five to seven miles an hour. During the time we have been in this stream, no paddling has been necessary except for the purpose of avoiding obstructions. At 9 we made our exit from this "cut off" and again entered the main river, where but little current was found. Width of river fifty yards and bank twelve to fifteen feet high for a short distance, when it falls to six and eight feet. For several miles we passed through country similar to that seen in the cut off, and covered with high grass and willow, and being miles in extent from the river as well as along its banks. At 1.30 we stopped at a plantation, cut some sugar cane— picked up some lemons and again moved on. (When the word *plantation* is used, do not think it refers to thousands of acres, as they vary in size from *one to ten acres*.) Distant mountains have been visible on our left during the entire day, but at this place they come to the water's edge. While passing through the cut off we saw thousands of Iguanas, and many birds of all kinds known to this section, except ducks of which but few were seen; and alligators constantly plunging into the water or swimming along the bank.

At 5 o'clock, our boatmen beginning to talk about camp, a promise of tobacco if we reached the bar that evening induced them to keep the paddles in motion, and our trip ended precisely at 6 o'clock. Having made the trip in 26 1-2 hours running time. We left San Pedro in the rain—slept in the rain last night—sat in the rain to-day from time of leaving camp to 2 P.M., and we are cold and disagreeable in the extreme. The fires that were visible as we approached the bar had a very comfortable appearance, and the chilly wind blowing from the sea caused us to seek their warmth at a double quick. We found a norther prevailing at the time of reaching the bar, and a very heavy sea running and breaking on the beach with tremendous force, which renders it impossible for boats to cross the bar and to go to Cienagueta. In crossing the bar one of the boats containing baggage was swamped, wetting all it contained, and ruining many articles. A courier left San Pedro on the morning of the 14th for this place but has not yet arrived, though he expected to come through in one day. He is doubtless at Cienagueta, awaiting a change in the weather, which will probably not occur for several days. Thermometer, 6 A.M. 68: 12 A.M. 71 1-2: 6 P.M. 79.

FEBRUARY 17th.—Rain again this morning—wind continuing and sea as rough as yesterday. All seem to be in doubt as to the best course to pursue, and find it difficult to decide whether it would be best to try the river as far as the "Cow Pen," (beyond which there are five shoals with only one foot water on them) or to return to Cienaqueta and try the mountains. By 9 A.M. the wind changed to the north-west, with an occasional shower, and the sun showing himself at noon, all hands engaged in drying wet clothing and other effects, which had been nearly completed on the previous day by Messrs. P. and F. It having been decided to try the river, preparation was at once commenced for the trip; two dories were engaged for the purpose, one of which when loaded will draw twenty inches and the other sixteen. This movement will be carried out unless information is received from San Pedro to stop it. Nothing heard of the courier. Thermometer 6 A.M., 68; 12 M., 71; 6 P.M., 70.

FEBRUARY 18th.—Rain again this morning, with heavy clouds at the north and west which present an angry appearance. Our blankets were wet again last night by the rain beating through our Cahoon shelters. After considerable exertion and great waste of patience we succeeded in making a fire, which we find as necessary for warmth as for culinary purposes, and perhaps more so, as the stock of provisions is not in great variety and the services of a Soyer is not needed in the kitchen. At 9.30 wind changed to the south, with rain falling heavily, and but little prospect of abatement. The natives cooked a Baboon to-day, but we know nothing of its flavor. We have eaten Conch, Iguana, and other things that did not present a very inviting *appearance,* but *no Baboon.* At 1 P.M. wind changed to the west—the rain ceased, and we again made a fire and dried, or attempted to dry what had again received a wetting. At night, the clouds disappeared, as usual. The sea continues very rough, and the roaring of the surf as it lashes the beach might be heard for several miles. Thermometer 6 A.M., 67; 12 M., 69; 6 P.M., 69.

FEBRUARY 19th.—To our great joy the sun rose clear this morning, and we feel anxious to make a start, but must wait for men from Cienagueta.

It is always delay with these people, who have no idea of the value of time, except as a means of measuring distance from one point to another. The sea being smoother this morning, a boat started for Omoa for provision for the men in charge of the effects of passengers who came by the last trip of the Steamer. Their effects are in bad order, having been wet for several days. Our individual baggage was returned from this place to Omoa, by the boat, we expect to leave San Pedro immediately on our arrival there, for the United States. The courier that left San Pedro on the morning of the 14th reached here at 10.30 A.M., having been detained at Cienagueta by bad weather, as we expected. The men expected from Cienagueta arrived in time to load the boats and be off by 1.45, P.M. They are to receive for transporting three thousand pounds of freight from here to the "Cow Pen," a distance of sixty-seven miles, forty-three dollars, payment to be made in currency, which is not greenbacks. The river was ascended for about eight miles, and camp pitched for the night. Thermometer 6 A.M., 65; 12 M., 73; 6 P.M., 71.

FEBRUARY 20th.—At 6 this morning we were again on the way, which is an early start for these people, though we should have been off an hour or more earlier. The bank at this place is three feet high, with plenty of Cahoon, and soil exceedingly rich. At 7 the heavens were overcast with "Mackerel Sky" which is a very good sign of rain, and the growling of a Baboon which was heard before we left camp, was pronounced by one of the boatmen a certain indication of a "falling weather." At 7.55 a point was passed where a raft will soon be formed, as the passage is only ten yards, while the stream is seventy-five yards in width; fallen trees having nearly closed it. The large boat got across the first log that has retarded our progress, at 8.40, when a line was taken ashore and in a few minutes she was off. By 9 the sky was perfectly clear, which was cheering, as we have no tarpaulins with which to cover our effects, and if they again get wet it will be a more serious undertaking to dry them than was the case at the bar. At 11 the plantation was reached where we obtained lemons on our down trip, and we again stopped to lay in a supply of plantains, lemons and sugar-cane. Our large boat stuck on a log at 3 P.M., but was not detained more than five minutes—the men taking water and dragging her off. In consequence of our being near the grassy region, and the terminus of Cahoon growth on this side of the "cut off," stopped at 4 and pitched camp, where it will be necessary to cook rations for two days, as we will soon be in a country where it will be almost impossible to find a camp. To-morrow we will be in the cut-off, when the *work of the trip* will begin. Thermometer 6 A.M., 60; 12 M., 76; 6 P.M., 74.

FEBRUARY 21st.—We are afloat this morning at 5:30, which is an improvement on yesterday's start. A heavy fog hangs over the river and it is quite cool. The cut off was entered at 9 A.M., the boat occupied by Captain B. and myself going ahead, as we have the pilot. The boats are all provided with poles and paddles, the first being constantly used after we left the river. Our boat camped at 5.40, near a place where the current was very swift, which point was not reached by the other boats; the large one camping three-fourths of a mile below us, and the cedar boat lower down. Thermometer 6 A.M., 63; 12 M., 80; 6 P.M., 78.

FEBRUARY 22d.—The large boat reached our camp at 6.40 this morning, and stopped to prepare provision for the day. The cedar boat is not in sight, yet we are not anxious concerning it as the men in charge have shown great energy, and one of them is the best boatman of the party. At 7.20, all hands having breakfasted we were again on the way. At 10.40 we reached our camp of the first night going down. Considerable detention was caused at 12 M. by the large boat getting across another log, which occurred again at 12.45. This log had to be cut in order to effect a passage. We are making very slow progress against the current, logs, stumps, vines and the overhanging branches of trees. At 3.20, our pilot finding we were in a lagoon, and consequently out of our course, it became necessary to turn back a mile in order to re-gain the right direction. We had hoped to be out of this flat country and once more among Cahoon, before night, but now think there is little chance of our doing so. At 5 P.M. the large boat grounded, and was relieved by all hands taking to the water and manning the gunwales. Camp was pitched this evening at 5.30, in a very disagreeable place, the cedar boat being a short distance ahead and the large boat about one hundred yards below us. Thermometer 6 A.M., 63; 12 M., 79 1-2; 6 P.M. 76.

FEBRUARY 23d.—6 o'clock found us on the way this morning, and we think from our locality we are about two miles from the main stream. At 6.15 the big boat was stopped by a log which it was found necessary to cut under water, and was again halted by a similar cause at 6.45, in a very rapid current. At 7.20 we reached a point where the river is almost entirely closed by a large tree lying across it, the only passage being a circular one worn by the current around the roots, which the large boat was *exactly large* enough to pass. At 8.05 all three boats were at the mouth of the cut-off, and in half an hour entered the Chamlicon, over a very rough place, tied up to rest for a few minutes, and again moved on. While our boat was being quietly poled along, at 10.50, the boy leaped into the water, and after a momentary scuffle, rose to the surface with a turtle weighing about eight pounds. We could see no indication of anything of the kind, and the water was not clear enough for the bottom to be seen. This beats any fishing we have seen, and proves a decided independence of hook and line. Our boat reached the Cow-pen at 4 P.M., the large boat at 5, but the cedar boat did not come up to-night. Thermom., 6 A.M., 63; 12 M. 79; 6 P.M. 76.

FEBRUARY 24th.—Captain Buckner and myself left Camp this morning for San Pedro, at 6.30. A note was discovered here last evening written by Col. H., who was here on Saturday (22d), which states the distance to San Pedro to be twelve miles. For several miles after leaving the Cow-pen our route lay over a rolling country; after which we came to a piece of prairie land with here and there a clump of small live oaks. This piece seemed to contain about two hundred acres, and is covered with coarse grass from two to three feet high. This being a high, dry, and rolling piece of ground, we asked ourselves the question, was this ever in cultivation? This trip will long be remembered by Captain B. and myself, as we left camp with baggage enough for a pack-mule of small dimensions, and though we slung it to a pole, and tried the shoulders, and this hand and that, keeping step with military precision, we failed to lessen its specific gravity. *En route*, the Blanca and Tacomiche were waded, the first two feet, and the second one foot deep, and we reached San Pedro at a late hour in the afternoon, where terminated one of the most fatiguing trips in which it was ever our misfortune to engage. Distance from S. Pedro to Cow-pen, thirteen miles, and from Cow-pen to bar, sixty-seven; total distance eighty miles. We will have occasion to refer to the river again. Thermometer, 6 A.M., 66; 12 M. 82; 6 P.M. 78.

FEBRUARY 25th.—A party is on the road between San Pedro and the Cow-pen, cutting the way wide enough for wagons, which is necessary to be done in a few places. Col. H. is with them to point out where certain advantageous changes may be made, as he examined the road a few days since. Thermometer, 6 A.M. 70; 12 M. 82; 6 P.M. 72.

FEBRUARY 26th.—As we expected, the man engaged yesterday to go to the Cow-pen for our baggage did not get off till this morning. *Extra* payment induced an earlier start than they are in the habit of making, and exacted the promise to be back this evening. He may arrive before morning and enable us to get off as we desire—but, patience! "We will see what we will see." A native was found last evening secreted in the house of an immigrant, and was tried, sentenced and punished by 12 M. to-day—receiving one hundred strokes with stout tamarind switches; in addition to which he will be required to work for the public a given length of time. *Mardi Gras* has been in operation here for the past two weeks, and on Monday last the *Trudor* [*Tudor?*] sports would have begun, which are carried to a considerable extent in Brazil by throwing flour on each other, and by throwing against the person their waxen bottles filled with scented water. We saw no flour used in that, or in any other manner, but a few persons used a small compressible metal bottle, throwing the water by squeezing the bottle. The individual who went for our baggage, returned this evening, which is wonderful indeed; but the person engaged to carry it to Omoa says he cannot start till day after to-morrow. We will endeavor to remove every obstacle to his going. Thermometer 6 A.M. 69; 23 M. 82; 6 P.M. 70.

FEBRUARY 27th.—Our baggage is ready, but not until the sun was an hour high did the party engaged to carry it make his appearance. He came to get money with which to purchase rations, Mr. D.S. having promised to feed him on the road, and also raised the price he at first charged, from two dollars to two dollars and fifty cents. Twenty-five cents being given him to procure rations, the work of tying on *two trunks* was commenced, three persons being engaged in it, which was completed to their satisfaction in half an hour. Ropes always have to be furnished for this purpose by the owner of baggage. Mr. Lucius Middlebrook and Mr. D.S. made a start at 8.10, and the baggage man at 8.30; we leaving San Pedro at 9.45, and overtaking the other gentlemen before they reached the mountain, the ascent of which was begun at 2.25 and terminated at Rancho Grande, at its foot, without accident, at 5.15 P.M.

The following being posted at Rancho Grande, is copied for the benefit of "all whom it may concern."

For ranging beast per night . . . . 6¼cts.
For use of bed with net (no bedding is furnished, C.S.) 50
" " without net 25
One meal at regular meal hours 37½
After 7 at night, each meal, each person 50
One cup of coffee, with biscuit 12½
Those who do not wish to occupy beds, may have the free use of the Hall.
(Signed) . . . . REGINO PREO, Proprietor

FEBRUARY 28.—At 6 this morning, we again mounted our mules and moved in the direction of the coast, congratulating ourselves on the fact of this being the last day over this miserable road. The day proved cloudy and without rain, which made the trip much more pleasant than would have been the case under a clear sky. We reached Omoa at 2.10, and the Judge's dinner hour being 4 P.M. we repaired to the Omoa river to exterminate the last *agarrapata.*

FEBRUARY 29th.—We engaged passage, and embarked on schooner Omoa, bound for Belize, at 1.15. During the afternoon and that night hardly a breath of air stirred, and we could not tell whether we were moving. Mr. D.S. has another chill, and we can only hope he will be as fortunate as on a former occasion, and have but one.

MARCH 1st.—No breeze to-day except of the most gentle character, and we are yet a long distance from our destination. The sun again disappeared beneath the horizon without our seeing Belize, though the trip is often made in twelve hours.

MARCH 2d.—Belize is in sight this morning, and we came to anchor at 12.30. A customhouse officer came aboard immediately, and permitted us to go ashore at once. We "put up" at Brewer's Hotel, Captain T. C. Brewer, proprietor. It affords us pleasure to be able to say the captain is an ex. Confed. and a gentleman, and that you will always find the *table d'Hôte* supplied with the best the market affords, and at reasonable rates. The sleeping apartments are neat, airy and comfortable. Patronize him if you visit Belize, and you will not go away dissatisfied.

MARCH 3D.—Jas. M. Putnam, Esq., agent for Messrs. Young, Toledo & Co., extended an invitation to us to accompany him to the Moho river, or rather the "Cattle Landing," two miles north of the mouth of that river, for which place he expects to start this evening with the steamer Enterprise, belonging to the firm mentioned, and will carry down a number of persons who arrived on the last steamer from New Orleans. We made our preparation for going, but the vessel did not make her appearance during the day.

MARCH 4th.—It is ascertained that the Enterprise is aground at the "Haul Over," which is a water connection between the Belize river and the Bay. The steamer had been in the river for some time undergoing repairs, and could only enter the Bay by the route named, on account of a bridge spanning the river in town. Quite a number of gentlemen who were waiting here for her, are gone this morning to tender their services in getting her off. Thermom. 6 A.M. 79; 12 M. 83; 6 P.M. 79.

MARCH 5th—The "Enterprise" succeeded in getting off the bar this morning and reached her anchorage in the harbor at 7.20 A.M. The "Trade-wind" will sail on the 7th, and we have abandoned the trip to the Moho, as it is two [sic] late for us to make it and return in time for the steamer, the distance being ninety miles. We paid our respects this morning to his Excellency, Gov. Longdon, and spent an hour both pleasantly and profitable with the gentleman. Having been informed of a grant made to an American Company, of an extensive piece of country lying between Monkey and Deep rivers, we made inquiry of his Excellency concerning it and found it was not as bad as we had heard. The "Enterprise" sailed this evening at 6, with a large company. Thermometer 6 A.M., 77; 12 M., 81; 6 P.M. 76.

MARCH 6th.—Several gentlemen on their way to the States arrived at Belize this morning from San Pedro. They informed us that a party had visited the Ulna river at its nearest point to San Pedro, eighteen miles, and that they reported six feet water to the bar of that stream. How they arrived at that conclusion we are unable to say, as we were not told they descended the river. We remember distinctly that, before we descended the Chemlicon it was reported to have two and a half feet at its lowest stage. Thermometer 6 A.M., 77; 12 M., 80; 6 P.M. 79.

MARCH 7th.—The wind has been blowing briskly from the east for several days, and we anticipated rough weather on the trip, but having made every preparation for the voyage, hope to pass the time more comfortably than from New Orleans here. The "Trade-wind" weighed anchor at 12 M., and we are off for the land of *Leafless trees*. At 1.25, in consequence of roughness of the sea on the "outside" cast anchor and remained here till morning. Thermometer 6 A.M., 77; 12 M., 81; 6 P.M., 78.

MARCH 8th—Anchor was weighed this morning at 6, and we are again on our way. In a few hours we were useless to ourselves, and of no service to any one, and might have been found occupying the upper berth in No. 9, which we kept not only to-day, but the next, and *the next*.

MARCH 11TH.—We are able to be up to-day, but feel as though we had passed through a severe attack of sickness. We think a roe herring would be good—none to be obtained—cranberry jelly—none within reach. "Waiter, have you any mackerel?" "I believe it is *all* gone, sir, but will see." "Mackerel, sir!" "Ah, thank you." Better mackerel we never ate, and a good breakfast was made though the quantity eaten was very small. Tried a cigar but succeeded in making a very small quantity of ashes. Took a chew, nauseating weed! how can any one use it? We retire to our room, lie down, and endeavor to decide which would be worse as a punishment for a person who is liable to sea-sickness—a compulsory sea faring life, the penitentiary, or decapitation. . . .

MARCH 12th.—Crossed the bar at 9.30 A.M., and reached New Orleans at 10 P.M., remaining on board till morning.

MARCH 13th.—By 12.30 baggage was delivered, and we are busy getting ready for the Jackson cars, which are to leave at 4 P.M. instead of 7, as was the case a short time since. We succeeded in making a start, and will reach "Old Warren," at 10.30, on the morning of March 14, 1868.

Insertion, pp. 121–125 in original

CONCLUSION

Though it would be pleasant to continue these pages, and give a more detailed account of the fruits, vegetables and mineral of the lands we visited, yet, feeling that we have already written too much to simply convey an idea of the country, must draw to a close. It has been our purpose from beginning to end, to give a fair and candid statement of *facts,* and to endeavor to enable all, *to see as we saw,* feeling satisfied they can draw satisfactory inferences therefrom. Much has been written concerning Honduras, that presented the appearance of speculation, and not unfrequently *by Speculators,* and comparatively little information of a detailed character has been given, which induced us to adopt a plan that we hope will not fail to convey a better idea of the country than has up to this time been attainable without making a trip. This, to the best of our ability, we have endeavored to do, even at the risk of repetition.

Whatever may be the pecuniary condition of people, we saw no one in Honduras, who left the United States, whose condition in that respect appeared enviable, and met but one person who had more money than he arrived there with. On the contrary, the emigrant lives in the simplest manner, and we were informed by a gentleman at San Pedro, who was in a position of independence once in the States, that for many days his family had not been provided with meat, and that he had no money even to purchase many articles of prime necessity, much less one of luxury—though beef can be bought for three cents per pound and pork at the same price. It is true a very great mistake was made at San Pedro, in planting cotton to the almost entire exclusion of every thing else, and the crop being destroyed by the Army Worm, and all their means being exhausted, they were compelled through necessity to exercise the most rigid economy. Very few have thus far erected houses, and are now paying for buildings of one room from 5 to 8 dollars a month.

It has been said of both British and Spanish Honduras, that certain crops can be made of a given quantity, and two crops in a year *without cultivation.* This brings up for consideration the fitness of those countries for agricultural and Horticultural purposes. We have already stated there is much good land to be found, but we saw a much larger proportion than we expected of what seemed very sandy. All seeds and plants must be planted at the commencement of, or during the rainy season, which in a great measure prevents cultivation on account of rain, if continuous, and we are of the opinion that if cultivation is carried to the same extent it was in the States before the war, and all grass and seeds removed, the sun will in many localities so parch the soil, that but little will be produced where much may be expected. This is not liable to be the case with sugar-cane, rice, the plantain nor banana; the first two covering the ground with a mass of vegetation, and the last two entirely shading it round the trees with their broad leaves and thereby retaining moisture in the earth. It is the custom with the natives to cultivate a piece of ground for one or two years, and then to clear another field, and abandon the first, as it is often easier to clear a new piece than the old, on account of the growth which makes its appearance on a field that has been planted being more difficult to remove.

Another reason was given by those who have had experience in cultivating that soil, which was, that in a very few years the soil becomes exhausted to some extent, and it would prove more profitable to change. How will it be with sugar-cane, that (as is the case with all plants containing saccharine matter), draws very heavily on the soil? In Honduras there is no rest for land that is planted in cane, for as soon as a cane is cut another springs up regardless of season, and we would ask, will not this constant and excessive drain soon exhaust one or more constituent elements of the soil, necessary to the growth of the plant? There is no land so rich that it will never become poor, and good cultivators of the soil have always found it to be profitable to rotate crops, and to feed their land before it becomes hungry and to rest it before it became weary. In the United States, vegetation is killed by frost, but in Honduras there is a constant growth of something on the soil, which is greater on land under tendance than on that covered with its primeval growth.

There can be no question that the "Eternal Summer" which prevails in Honduras will be monotonous to a degree that will prove anything but pleasant. To us, autumn has ever been the most interesting season of the year, "the sere and yellow leaf" indicating a repose of the vegetable kingdom, and never failed to awaken thoughts of a pleasant character, and feelings of reverence. The sighing of the winds of winter through the lattice, the cheerful fireside, with the domestic scene it is unnecessary to describe, make a picture most of us are familiar with, but is lost, forever lost to the emigrant in Honduras, though it can never be forgotten. The beautiful scenery constantly before the eye at San Pedro, must in the course of time lose its novelty, and cease to impress the mind as at first, and draw forth on certain occasions remarks of a similar character to one we heard from a gentleman who had for some time resided in Honduras which was "We can not live on beautiful scenery." What a volume was expressed in these few words, and in the mournful manner in which they were uttered! In conversations with old residents of Belize, they invariably expressed their surprise at persons locating on the coast of that country, which they stated had been attempted from time to time, without profit or health attending the honest and persistent efforts of those who selected that portion of the country.

Most of those persons who left this country with the view of making Honduras their future home, did so because of the unsettled condition of affairs at the South, and under belief that any clime would prove better than the one they were leaving, on which point a very great mistake has been made, and we undertake to say without hesitation, that a large number would return at once if they were in possession of sufficient means to enable them to do so. Many on leaving their home either "swore in their wrath," or affirmed in their agony that they would never return, which will keep them away, whatever obstacles they may be called upon to remove, or privations they may have to endure. We have in our mind's eye several gentlemen of education, great energy, and influence, who are in this position, and will they not succeed in keeping many in the country who if left to exercise their own judgement would leave at an early day? While many are leaving the "land of their birth," because of the character of the Government under which they are living, or we might say the almost entire absence of Government, would it not be well, first to examine into the character of the Government they are about to remove to? And on the point of social equality, which is to some a hideous phantom, that at times threatens to assume the density of solid, would it not be well to exercise a little thought before packing up?

In closing, we indulge the hope that if hereafter any should select the countries of Central America in order to benefit their condition, that they need not necessarily undertake the movement without some information that will be more valuable to them than any we were able to obtain before leaving New Orleans. And if we are the means of preventing disappointment or suffering, even to a limited extent, our purpose will be more than accomplished, and our most sanguine expectations realized. While we give no advice, having studiously avoided doing, so, we would regret to hear of persons leaving this country without sufficient means to enable them to return. For to be thrown upon a distant shore, among people with whom we have few thoughts or feelings in common, and to be compelled to remain, if a favorable impression is not made, is a condition we have never experienced, and cannot describe, but which would be anything but pleasant, particularly if women and children should be of the number. Our task is done, and we can honestly say was undertaken more for the purpose of benefiting our fellow citizens than for any other reason, and in accordance with what many friends have been pleased to call the exercise of a Christian duty.

THE END

Part III

Community Failures, Black Migration, and Charles Swett after 1868

✳

Overall, Charles Swett's pamphlet gave good advice. The vast majority of the colonies created by former Confederates did not work out. We have described Vila Americana in Brazil, Toledo in British Honduras, and the Coleman family in Honduras. That is not much to show for the scale of many Confederates' initial aspirations.

Why was there such dramatic and unrelenting failure? There were some common structural features of the entire endeavor that condemned most of the colonies to failure. The two most important of the Confederates' problems revolved around race and labor. But even apart from these issues, many of the Confederate exiles were not very good guests in their adopted country nor did many of them attempt to fit into civil society. In Mexico, the Carlota colony was a rowdy and turbulent place riven by internal dissention and scorned by its Mexican neighbors. And we have seen that locals, black and white, resented the former Confederates' behavior in British Honduras.

THE ISSUE OF RACE

The problem of race meant that the Confederates in Brazil and British Honduras had to isolate their settlements from the host societies in order not to be contaminated by local customs and laws that, to degrees thought intolerable by the U.S. Southerners, granted citizenship rights and opportunities for people of African descent.

Vila Americana in Brazil was an example of a community that managed to cut itself off from most of Brazilian society, but not as completely as many residents desired. By the 1880s competition by neighboring Italian immigrant families drove Vila Americana farmers out of the watermelon market. Racial and cultural exclusivity does not appear to have survived more than a couple of generations. Confederate battle flags notwithstanding, one scholar in the 1930s observed that "around Vila Americana there was little evidence of Confederate blood in the veins of the inhabitants." Sixty years later an Italian visitor described the great extent to which the descendants of the Vila Americana Confederates had intermarried and assimilated into Brazilian society.[1] And as we have seen, the strength and severity of Methodism in Toledo, British Honduras, isolated the community from even its Confederate colleagues. In the cases of both Vila Americana and Toledo, the extent to which the communities managed to detach themselves from their host societies must have exacted high costs and weakened their ability to respond flexibly to the vagaries of weather, illness, politics, and other challenges.

More to the point, if the object was to re-create or preserve the Southern way of life, race and class hierarchies had been a critical feature of the ethos of the planter elite. Ideally, the Southern way of life required subordinated people to occupy permanently low stations and to do the most distasteful work. Visual markers, such as skin color, as well as class and cultural differences are useful for maintaining and reproducing caste structures. The Confederate version of the good society required racial and class subordination in Southerners' newly created communities to replicate their former lives; in what amounted to a frontier existence without slavery, these requirements were difficult to achieve.

LABOR SCARCITY

Who was going to do the work in these communities? Swett did not elaborate much on this issue. Occasionally he observed, with admiration and a sense of wonderment, that men who had relatively little experience with manual labor were willing to live as pioneers (for example, January 2 and 12). His only mention in the diaries of the availability of "natives" to work for the immigrants concerned the preparation of weather boarding and not agricultural labor (January 12). Only in the appendix does Swett note the scarcity of labor available for hire in both British Honduras and Spanish Honduras. This turned out to be one of the most critical issues for all Confederate emigrants.

In Brazil, very few ex-Confederates arrived with sufficient resources to buy a working plantation with slaves. Even if a colonist in British Honduras or Honduras had the resources, slavery had been eliminated in both places for decades. Moreover, the slave trade was illegal even when slavery was not, as in Brazil and Cuba, and when colonists tried to take former slaves abroad as "servants," they were unsuccessful. For example, General Thomas C. Hindman, commander of the Trans-Mississippi army before Kirby-Smith, wrote from Mexico that "all our Negroes decided to leave us upon our arrival here, and did so, except Charlie, whom I employed until I could get Mexican servants. He will leave tomorrow."[2] These acts of free will were similar to that exercised by William Owens, whom Swett had identified as "an 'American citizen of African descent,' who accompanies Col. H. to serve him in the capacity of cook, being an old servant of the Colonel" (January 6). On January 27 William Owens, "our *chef de cuisine*," left Honduras without Colonel Harrison to return to Louisiana. Although he said that he wanted to return and might recruit others to come with him, there is no indication that he ever did.

One possibility was to bring in workers so desperate that they could be subjected to direct coercion although they were not officially slaves. The British Honduras Company's experiment with Chinese workers was a debacle. The other large pool of terribly impoverished workers was India, but apart from the Sepoy mutineers who were "transported" in the late 1850s, the British government never sponsored the large-scale postemancipation immigrations of South Asians to British Honduras that it did to Trinidad and British Guyana. The Toledo community in 1872 had sufficient resources to pay labor contractors in Jamaica to bring indentured South Asian workers to work in their sugarcane fields. Although the South Asian workers were, technically, low-paid wageworkers, Toledo employers were able to hold them as virtual prisoners and impose slavelike conditions on them. Nevertheless, the South Asians' survival rates were higher than those of the contracted Chinese workers. Sugar production did rise in Toledo but at a time when the price of sugar was disastrously low due to the rapid growth of cheap European beet sugar production. A market survival strategy, practiced by many sugarcane producers at this time, was to make use of sugarcane's singular advantage over sugar beets—that is, to make rum. This was not an option, however, for the strict Protestants in the Toledo community, despite their "un-Christian" treatment of their Hindu and Muslim workers.[3]

The employment of contracted, indentured labor required a substantial initial outlay that was beyond the financial means of most immigrants and their communities. Hiring local wage labor was a second possibility, but remained difficult. Labor was in short supply, and ex-Confederates at home and abroad were still adjusting to supervising workers as employees and not as slaves. British Hondurans of African descent simply would not put up with white Southerners' attitudes toward them, much less the harsh working conditions and low pay offered by the Southerners.

In British Honduras, this left the indigenous peoples, especially those to the south and west of the city of Belize ("Mayans"). Although British Honduras had the legal framework for debt peonage, the colony did not have the enforcement mechanisms necessary to turn debt peonage into the kind of coercive labor system that emerged in Guatemala coffee production in the 1870s.[4] So instead of a coercive debt peonage system, the Southerners often found themselves making an advance of wages to establish a debtor relationship only to have the workers disappear almost immediately with the advances. The Toledo community petitioned the lieutenant governor in 1868 for a magistrate and police in order to enforce labor contracts, but to no apparent effect.[5]

In San Pedro Sula, there were simply so few people in the region in the mid-nineteenth century that there were, for all practical purposes, no wageworkers. Charles Swett emphasized the scarcity of labor for hire, and even if someone were to agree to work for a wage, "The price usually paid for men, field hands, is from five to seven dollars per month and their provision, and from eight to ten when they feed themselves." While domestic help was cheaper, it was beyond the means of most, if not all colonists. He notes that "as is the case in British Honduras, laborers and servants *are scarce*, and the few to be found are seldom anxious to hire. We do not know of a family of immigrants at San Pedro provided with native servants, they doing their work in most cases themselves." (The quotations are from Appendix B.)

This points to one of the central contradictions of the emigration endeavor. The existence of plentiful, unclaimed land in British Honduras, Brazil, Honduras, and Venezuela made it possible for the exiles to settle there. At the same time, the seeming emptiness of this land was precisely the condition that did *not* provide a ready, willing, and cheap agricultural labor force. Without slavery or debt peonage, disgruntled workers could simply fade away to other kinds of opportunities or open up farms for themselves. When there was a greater density of population, there was a different dynamic, but not necessarily a positive one. In Mexico, people were thrown off the land to make room for the colonists. This might have been a first step in creating a pool of people with few or no alternatives to working for low wages, but the danger was that local hostility toward the migrant communities could lead to their destruction.

CONTRADICTIONS OF HOMESTEADING

The vast majority of the Confederate emigrants to Brazil, British Honduras, and Honduras were forced to use family labor in the homesteading tradition to clear the land, build houses, and plant, harvest, and transport a product. Overcoming adversity through hard work had been a source of pride for the first generation of Mississippians in the 1830s, and some Confederates evoked this tradition as they settled into physical toil in order to escape Reconstruction. Josephine Foster, a young woman who had migrated from Mississippi to Mexico to Brazil, proudly expressed this sentiment in a letter to the editor of the *New Orleans Times*, published on April 26, 1868:

> I have known ["a certain class that *hard work* does not agree with"] to
> . . . go to Rio de Janeiro for the purpose of meeting their families, and
> return with them to the United States on the next steamer. Everything
> they have said in praise of Brazil and Brazilians seems to fade away in
> the distance when they are thoroughly convinced that *manual labor*
> is the one thing needful to help us on to a fortune in this country. It
> really seems that they straightway commence fabricating some ter-
> rible tale to justify themselves in returning to the States, that they
> so recently left with bitter curses. In a little while such people leave
> in disgust with *colored equality*, as they term it, and return to *negro
> superiority*.[6]

Foster's attitude aside, the homesteading labor model did not work for the vast majority of the Southern immigrants. In order to have any hope of success, families had to satisfy some predictable stringent requisites. They had to become used to manual labor, know how to do what had to be done in a new terrain and climate, have sufficient funds to keep themselves for at least a year without income, and be physically robust enough to survive long hours of hard work, primitive living conditions, and frequent expo-sure to illness. The vast majority of the exiles could not manage, for all the reasons we have discussed, to put these ingredients together in the rugged and inhospitable environment of their newly adopted countries.

But the problems lay deeper than the ability to survive. Even when peo-ple worked hard enough and well enough to get by, this success was at the expense of the values and aspirations underlying the emigration effort. First of all, homesteading was not a social organization of production consistent with an aristocratic social formation. The lack of a distinct, subordinated group of workers and dependence on family labor made for, at least to some extent, more egalitarian communities. Egalitarianism violated aristocratic

Southern ideas about class boundaries, a reaction that surfaced in the Confederate communities in Mexico. The Mexican communities, because of their origins in panicked flight, probably contained a more representative cross section of the U.S. South's white society and more persons outside the planter elite than most of the others. In Carlota, former governors, generals, and planters complained about the lack of customary types of deference shown them by fellow whites.[7]

In more general terms, those in even the most successful and durable Confederate exile communities did not find themselves living lives consistent with the ideal of antebellum plantation life in the U.S. South. Nonetheless, they inadvertently succeeded in re-creating a significant component of life past and present in the South. The bitter fact was that living in these exile communities, at best, entailed a lifestyle disturbingly like that of poor Southern whites. The ex-Confederates were certainly not aspiring to an identity based on the lives of poor whites when they emigrated, but it was usually the best that they could achieve.[8]

The former Confederates' retreat from the countrysides of Brazil, British Honduras, and Honduras and the exodus back to the United States accelerated after 1870. In Brazil, much more so than in British Honduras and Honduras, some immigrants moved from agrarian pursuits into towns and cities and made livings in business and the professions and were assimilated into the mainstream of Brazilian society. Many immigrants did stay in Belize for a while, but it was because they did not have the money for a return passage, having lost whatever they had in their agricultural ventures or as victims of fraud. Destitute ex-Confederates roamed the streets posing a public safety problem, especially for the black citizenry. The U.S. consul's description of the demise of the Medina community in Honduras says that its members were destitute, but they "worked and begged their way back to their homes."[9]

Only a miniscule proportion of the voluntary exiles succeeded in establishing stable and lasting communities, and those who did were unable to replicate U.S. plantation life of the 1850s. When it looked as though a new labor system with substantial white control was emerging in the U.S. South and the likelihood of African Americans' full political and economic citizenship was receding, the lure of returning to the United States was irresistible. The reality was that the antebellum white version of the Southern ideal was becoming more feasible in the postbellum United States. Charles Swett had been right in his view that the planter class might once again be politically dominant. But the use of violence to achieve that dominance created strong incentives for African Americans to leave the South.

BLACK MIGRATION OUT OF THE SOUTH

The diaspora of former Confederates from the United States after the Civil War was not the only example of emigration linked to the aftermath of slavery. There was a significant history of voluntary African American emigration from the United States before the Civil War. The American Colonization Society, formed in 1816, was the principal initiator of expatriating free black men and women, and the society transported 11,000 people to Liberia in the forty years before the Civil War.[10] The society was not at first associated with the antislavery movement, and William Lloyd Garrison condemned the entire enterprise as a tactic to sustain U.S. slavery.

Nevertheless, it was not long before the society and its supporters did become closely identified with the conservative abolitionist movement that advocated the gradual, compensated emancipation of slaves and then sending them abroad but not necessarily to Liberia. Although some white Southerners were interested in ridding their region of free blacks and initially participated in the scheme, the growing abolitionist tendencies of the members of the American Colonization Society made the whole idea anathema to all but a few whites in the U.S. South before the Civil War.[11]

Southern whites' fear of freed African Americans and their pessimism about creating a new plantation system with free labor led some whites to propose colonizing (exiling) freed African Americans from the South, either to a foreign country or to isolated areas in the West.[12] But as Frederick Douglass and Secretary of State William Seward both argued, there were no real substitutes for African American agricultural workers in the South for the foreseeable future.[13]

By the middle of the 1870s Southern whites were making an aggressive return to social and political power based on the Mississippi plan—a strategy of terrorizing "uppity" ex-slaves, Northern teachers, and reformers. The federal government confirmed the triumph of the white Southern mission when it officially ended Reconstruction in 1877 and forbade federal troops from interfering in Southern affairs.[14] African Americans had been going back into the fields under new forms of labor control, tenant farming and sharecropping. Now exercising more political and economic control, and in need of the cheapest labor possible, planters and New South enthusiasts were opposed to black migration out of the United States. At the time black communities found that leaving the South was increasingly attractive, if not always practicable.

As they experienced violence by whites, growing political disenfranchisement, and continued economic oppression, large numbers of Southern

African Americans began to consider leaving the South. Liberia was one of the most frequently mentioned destinations, as can be seen by the formation of the Colonization Council in Louisiana (1876), the incorporation of the Liberian Exodus Joint-Stock Steamship Company in South Carolina (1877), and the inundation of the American Colonization Society with pleas from Southern blacks.[15] Although the Liberian Exodus Joint-Stock Steamship Company did manage to take 206 emigrants to Liberia in 1878, financial obstacles precluded a mass emigration. Even the trip to New York City to embark on an American Colonization Society ship was not financially feasible for the vast majority of Southern African Americans seeking to go to Liberia.

Kansas was another attractive site for migration. Abolitionist and temperance Republicans controlled Kansas, and although they did not make special provisions for Southern black migrants, they did not actively discriminate against them. Kansas authorities did not treat the Southern black migrants much differently from the thousands of white migrants from Ohio, Indiana, and Illinois also seeking federal homestead grants or inexpensive land being sold by the railroads as part of the railroads' federal subsidies. A few of the Southern black migrants went to other states, but in addition to the political climate and available land, Kansas had a positive symbolic value due to its association with John Brown and struggles for black freedom. Between March and May 1879—the height of the "Kansas Fever Exodus"—4,000 African Americans arrived in Kansas from Louisiana and Mississippi alone. The route to Kansas from northern Texas was shorter, and between November 1879 and May 1880, 3,000 to 4,000 blacks from Texas moved to Kansas. The 1880 Kansas census found over 28,000 African Americans who had been born in former slave states.[16]

Many more tried to go, but the lack of resources, together with white resistance, frustrated their attempts. When steamships refused to pick up black passengers along the Mississippi for almost a full month in April and May 1879, thousands of migrants were stranded on the banks of the river for weeks. These were poor, rural, black Southerners, and any transit delay ate into their scarce resources and could be life threatening. Another reaction by white Southerners to this exodus was to beat, jail, and occasionally kill people trying to migrate.

Black out-migration rekindled Southern whites' fear of labor scarcity and revived interest in encouraging immigration into the South to replace intractable and scarce workers. Such efforts in the immediate postwar years had not been successful. In the late 1870s a San Francisco labor contractor who received an inquiry about supplying Chinese laborers said that he could not supply Chinese workers for the wages paid African Americans.[17] Nevertheless, in the 1870s and 1880s several hundred Chinese workers were brought in to work in cotton and sugarcane fields. The problem was that the Chinese did not stay long on the plantations, preferring to become fishers or to migrate to cities and engage in commerce and the trades.[18]

CHARLES SWETT AND THE "LOST CAUSE"

Charles Swett went back to Mississippi after his return from British Honduras in 1868; he seems never to have seriously considered migrating to the Confederate communities that turned out so badly. No longer in the possession of a farmhouse, let alone his slaves, he abandoned the plantation idyll for the moment and took up the lumber business, probably drawing on some of the capital his father had accumulated at the hardware store in Vicksburg, now under the management of Daniel Swett's nephew from the North, Lee Richardson. Charles Swett's father, Daniel, retired to his farmland outside Vicksburg, where he and his wife died within six months of each other in 1878. Charles Swett took his own advice on the importance of Southerners joining the industrial economy in the postwar era. He moved southeast to Copiah County and opened a lumber mill and store outside the town of Beauregard, renamed for the famous Confederate general whom Swett had encountered in his role as artillery inspector.

The strategic location of the Swett hardware store in Vicksburg was not lost on Charles as he chose a new home in Mississippi. Copiah County is situated just to the east of the Illinois Central Railroad line, which opened the route from Chicago through Mississippi to New Orleans in 1857. By 1870 the county was a center of textile mill production, and the Mississippi Cotton and Woolen Mill in nearby Wesson, founded by Colonel J. M. Wesson in 1866, had become one of the largest textile mills in the South. Both the textile mills and the railroads were large consumers of milled lumber, one of Mississippi's most important industries in the 1870s and 1880s; by 1880 the state had 292 sawmills.[19]

Charles Swett and his growing family had made a reasonably quick recovery from the economic catastrophe of the war. By 1870 the census reported that his mill was worth $5,000 and that his personal property in Copiah County totaled $2,000. Swett also received ten patents between 1866 and 1873: eight for different ways to fasten cotton bales, one for an artificial leg, and one for fire tongs. His first patent was awarded in 1866, and he successfully defended it against infringement in 1871. These activities indicate perspicacity but also show how quickly Swett was willing to trust his fate to the federal patent and judicial systems. Daniel, his father, was not shy about utilizing U.S. government agencies, and he actively pursued recompense from the U.S. Office of the Commissioners of Claims for goods lost and services rendered to the Union army during the Civil War.[20]

Charles Swett was supporting a large establishment, and no doubt was working hard as a merchant, an occupation he had compared to slavery in his pamphlet. His growing family now included six children ranging in age from sixteen to two. His brother William Swett worked at the mill as a clerk, and Charles employed a "mulatto" teenager named John Richardson (perhaps his cousin's son) and two white teenagers as laborers. Olivia Clay, an illiterate fourteen-year-old African American girl, was probably a servant or a nursemaid. Beauregard had the dubious distinction of "state-wide notoriety for its size and number of saloons."[21] In 1883 a tornado leveled most of the town, but by then Charles and Amanda Swett and their children had returned to Warren County.

Amanda and Charles Swett may have viewed the move to Copiah County as a necessary but hopefully temporary evil. Both had strong family ties to Warren County, and Charles's sister, Caroline Louise, widowed in 1865, had married Amanda's brother, William Oates, a physician, in 1869. The death of both of Swett's parents in 1878 may have provided an inheritance that enabled him to close the mill and return to the quiet life of a gentleman farmer close to his and his wife's families.

The Swett family was doing well, although general economic recovery throughout the South was slow. More promising, in the view of whites, was their political recovery. Political support for Reconstruction in the North was waning. Many Republicans were frustrated by Reconstruction's expense and uncertain progress, and others simply saw new and more rewarding policy directions—supporting the rapid industrial and transportation developments inside and outside the South.[22] As a consequence of Northern lack of attention, whites' political power was restored at the state, county, and local levels, although they would not succeed in completely driving out African American officeholders until the late nineteenth and early twentieth centuries.

What would become a process of reconciliation and reunion between Northern and Southern whites was aided by the post–Civil War flood of soldiers' memoirs, especially those by generals from both sides of the conflict. These memoirs consistently stressed strategy, courage, the experience of the battle, and the high qualities of the enemy. After all, if you were to portray the enemy as weak and ineffectual, it would, on the one hand, diminish your achievement of winning the war, or, on the other hand, make you look still worse for losing it. The function of these memoirs' narrow focus and selectivity went beyond putting the author in a good light; memoirs played an important role in the process of reunion and reconciliation between whites in the North and South while erasing slave liberation and at the expense of black rights and opportunities.[23]

An important aspect of casting the Civil War in sentimental, chivalrous terms that rendered slavery invisible was white men's rhetorical veneration of white Southern women, most evident in effusive, cloying public speeches about the virtue and purity of white women. The Civil War could then be seen as having been fought to protect Southern white women from Yankees and especially from black men. While fulsome portrayals often lauded women's passive domesticity, we have already noted how many Southern white women were active participants in the war effort, and after the war they were the principal initiators of organizing Confederate commemorations and cemeteries. Charles Swett expressed his gratitude to this contribution when he dedicated his narrative of Swett's Battery to the Daughters of the Confederacy.

Whites in the U.S. North and West as well as the South were strongly attracted to romantic images of the Old South and of the bravery and principled loyalties of both Southern and Northern soldiers, and these emphases were consistent with recasting the reasons for the Civil War in Southern terms—that is, it was *not* about slavery and race.[24] Southern whites lost slavery and the right to secede, but they eventually restored crucial aspects of states' rights—the ability to disenfranchise blacks and to oppress them without interference from the federal government.

Celebrating white war dead was also integral to the process of reconciliation. While the Swetts were in Copiah County, their Warren County neighborhood had changed significantly. In Vicksburg, as elsewhere, black and white cemetery associations, often organized by women, were marking graves, decorating them with flowers and patriotic symbols, and pressuring state and federal governments to participate in honoring the Civil War dead. The Swett and Oates farms were close to the battlegrounds of the siege of Vicksburg and to the thousands of unidentified graves left in its wake. When the federal government declared the burial grounds of Vicksburg a national cemetery in 1866, it was constructed on the edges of the two families' farms.

Union and Confederate veterans were mobilizing around the country to hold reunions and build statues, monuments, and chapels, including white women in Vicksburg who raised money for the erection of a "battle abbey" to commemorate the Confederate dead. One result of this agitation was the federal government's passage of funding to build a national military park near the Vicksburg National Cemetery. Gettysburg, Chickamauga, and Shiloh had already been designated national parks. When the federal government purchased land for the military park in 1899 and 1900, it paid a flat per-acre rate. While whites could purchase new land with the proceeds from the sale at going rates, black farmers always had to pay high premiums to buy more land from whites who owned it. The director of land purchasing recognized and regretted this, but he was constrained by the budget and by the predictable political reactions among local whites if he were to pay blacks a higher price for their land.[25] The result was that several black farmers found themselves not only disenfranchised at the ballot box but also dispossessed of their farms.

Charles Swett attended Vicksburg reunions of Mississippi Confederate veterans and joint Confederate-Union gatherings. As the only known extant photograph of him testifies, he was still able to fit into his uniform after three decades. With Jim Crow firmly in place, black veterans, who had played a critical role in taking Vicksburg, were closed out of such celebrations except as servants. Nevertheless, blacks had their own commemorations in that part of the national cemetery where black Civil War dead were buried. In what became a national Memorial Day in late May, they customarily cleaned and decorated the graves and listened to a reading of Lincoln's Gettysburg Address.

When the enormous Illinois monument was dedicated in the Vicksburg park in 1906, a parade of Illinois and Mississippi veterans marched to the park, and Governor James K. Vardaman, known for his racist hatemongering, declared, "The men and women of the South believed that they had a constitutional right to do what they did."[26] It may have been this event that triggered Swett's decision to record his Civil War memories in 1908, two years before his death in 1910. In the Lost Cause tradition, he had fulsome praise for "that glorious organization," the Vicksburg chapter of what became the Daughters of the Confederacy, which hoped to bestow a Southern Cross of Honor on every Confederate veteran.

Historians such as David Blight and Christopher Waldrep have argued that by the time Swett wrote his memoir in 1908, whites in both the North and the South had forgotten slavery as a cause of the Civil War. With segregation and black disenfranchisement firmly in place, "reunion" of the sections was accomplished by disremembering what had caused the Civil War in the first place. Civil War veterans such as Swett, in fact, had not needed to flee the South for Mexico and Central and South America. With the

8. Charles Swett (1828–1910). He was seventy-seven years old at the time of the picture, attending a Civil War veterans' reunion in Vicksburg. Old Court House Museum, Vicksburg, Mississippi.

end of Reconstruction and the triumph of the Southern version of the war throughout the nation, they had, in effect, re-created the racial and political order that they so highly prized. Swett closed his 1908 memoir by declaring that "'The Civil War', or 'War between the States', closed so far as I was concerned, in 1865, and I can truthfully say, I entertain no feeling of animosity toward those who opposed me. . . . I am now an 'American Citizen.'"

Appendix A

Documents Concerning the Settlement of Medina, Honduras

✳

*W*e have rearranged the following documents from the pamphlet, presenting them in chronological order. Charles Swett reproduced both the
Spanish- and English-language versions of each of these documents, except
for numbers 4, 7, and 8, which were originally in English. The English versions of originally Spanish documents were translated in January and February 1868 by José Reynaud, the party's host. Some of the translations are,
well, rather loose, but we have inserted words in brackets in only a few places
where we believed it necessary.

LIST OF DOCUMENTS

Document 1. Congressional Decree from the *Legislative Bulletin* (March
14, 1866).

Document 2. "Agricultural Emigrants and Political Emigrants," *Gazeta Oficial*, vol. 6, no. 78.

Document 3. *A Municipal Act of the Authorities of San Pedro, for the Protection of Foreign Immigrants* (April 1867).

Document 4. Communication from Green Malcolm to His Excellency
the President and Executive Officers of the Republic of Honduras (May 3,
1867).

Document 5. Response by Ponciano Leiva Lopez, Minister of Interior Relations and Government of the Republic of Honduras, to Green Malcolm
(May 8, 1867).

Document 6. Ponciano Leiva Lopez, Minister of Interior Relations and Government of the Republic of Honduras, appoints Green Malcolm Inspector of Foreign Immigration (May 8, 1867).

Document 7. Declaration by Green Malcolm to municipal authorities of San Pedro Sula (February 24, 1868).

Document 8. Announcement of a resolution passed by the City Council of Medina (February 24, 1868).

Document 1.

The following is from the Legislative Bulletin of March 14th, 1866:

Comayagua, 14TH March 1866

The President of the Republic of Honduras

To its Inhabitants:

Be it known: That the Sovereign Congress has decreed the following:

"The Sovereign Congress, with the view of laying down the conditions under which Foreign Immigration is to be admitted into the Republic; and in compliance with article 19 of the Constitution, hereby

DECREES:

Art. 1. To all foreigners wishing to domiciliate in Honduras are granted the rights of the Natives under the laws, to which Immigrants shall be subject from the moment they acquire a domicil [sic].

Art. 2. The foreigner who, within five years from the day he obtains his certificate of residence, shall positively cultivate some national land, establishing thereon permanent farms, will thereby acquire the right of property to said land, and shall moreover have the right of taking from other contiguous Government lands such materials as may be necessary for the improvement of his place.

Art. 3. Foreigners shall enjoy the privilege of exemption from military service during a period of ten years, except in case of national war to repel invasion; and during four years shall not be required to perform any civil duty.

Art. 4. Immigrants whose religious creed may be different from the prevailing religion, may privately follow their own religion and erect cemeteries for the dead.

Art. 5. Immigrants shall not be subject, during eight years, to any [extraordinary] tax or impost, nor have to pay fiscal duties for the introduction of machinery, tools, instruments and books for the use of their professional or industrial pursuits.

Art. 6. The Executive Power shall grant exclusive privileges to foreigners who may invent or introduce machines, or useful improvements, not in use in this country.

Art. 7. At all times, foreigners free from all legal responsibility shall be at liberty to immigrate ["*emigrar*"—emigrate] and to dispose of their interests at their own will.

Art. 8. Immigrants who may take on lease private lands, or farms, shall not be required to pay higher contributions than is usually required from natives.

Art. 9. The benefits granted under this law are understood to extend also to immigrants from the Republics of America.

Given in the Session Hall of the National Congress. Comayagua, February 26, 1866. Juan Lopez, D. P.—Carlos Madrid, D. S.—Jeronimo Zelaya, D. S.

{SEAL.}

Document 2.

Knowing that the Official Gazette of all countries is supposed to reflect the sentiment of the Government, the following is inserted to give information that may be of value, or at least of interest to those who contemplate removing to Spanish Honduras.

(Extract from the 6th Volume, No. 78, of the "*Gazeta Oficial*" of Honduras)

AGRICULTURAL EMIGRANTS AND POLITICAL EMIGRANTS.

Our industry and civilization, so much in need of energetic, experienced and enterprising men ["The original says "*extrangeros pacíficos*"—peaceful foreigners, with no other adjectives], already begin to give unmistakable evidences of the immense benefits to be derived by our country from the advent and permanent settlement on our soil of the industrious and enlightened immigrants whom the liberal policy of our Government is now attracting to our shores, and whose labors, we have no doubt, will soon render available the hitherto hidden and unprofitable treasures of our fertile soil.

A considerable number of immigrants provided with capital and agricultural implements have already arrived from the United States, and the various plantations which here and there have sprung up under their care, promising a just reward for their labors, cannot fail to insure the continued influx of this desirable class of population. At the same time several contracts on foot for the building of the projected Inter-Oceanic Railroad, which will, when realized, change, as if by enchantment, the fate of this country now bound and compressed between two seas, for want of a railroad to establish communication between them.

The Republic, then, free from the recent troubles of the war of Olancho, has now reached a period when, under the auspices of peace and wise legislation, the incalculable resources of its soil will begin to develop.

Apart from the contracts which will be sanctioned by the next Congress, there is a law sufficiently liberal to attract foreign Immigration, and the Executive Power is authorized to increase the concessions. In fact, the law contains the best dispositions for the realization of this object; but under such prudent restrictions, that in no case, can the benefits and privileges thus conferred, be converted into a dangerous power in our midst.

It is therefore important for all parties to understand the true policy of the Government on this subject.

It is not in the spirit of that policy to tolerate the establishment of colonies that would assume the attitude of groups in which would prevail the solidarity of a dangerous foreignism.

Neither should it be interpreted as granting rights or privileges to certain nations, corporations or individuals, that would exclude others from the common benefits which the laws of the country offer to all peaceable immigrants from all parts of the world.

In relation to the Railroad, that plan will be most acceptable that shall give the best guarantee of practicability.

With regard to political emigrants from the neighboring Republics, the Government, much interested in the peace of Central America, will faithfully conform with the treaties which exist between some of them and this Government; and with respect to emigrants from those republics with whom we have as yet no treaty, they shall be dealt with according to the strictest principles of reason and equity; not permitting them in any case to exercise hostilities against their own government; but this, in such manner, that in cases not defined, the Constitution of the Republic shall not be infringed, for the President is determined to enforce at all times the provisions of that Instrument which he had the honor of sanctioning, without being at liberty to violate it.

Document 3.

On the 22d of April 1867 the Act given below was passed by the town of San Pedro for the protection of foreign Immigrants.

A Municipal Act of the Authorities of San Pedro, for the Protection of Foreign Immigrants.

I, Jse. Maria Merlo, Secretary of the Municipality of San Pedro, do herby [*sic*] certify:

That in the book of Acts and Resolutions, of the Municipality for this year, is found the Resolution which literally says:

Municipal Session Hall, San Pedro, April 22, 1867

The Municipality of San Pedro, in extraordinary session assembled, in conjunction with the Council and other citizens, presided by his Honor the Alcalde Municipal, and after hearing the petition presented by Col. Green Malcolm, a native of the United States of North America, representing the emigration from said States already arrived or that may hereafter arrive at this place, with the object of domiciliating here, for himself and in behalf of his associates, he solicits the right of settling among us, and also the grant of lands to build houses for residence, and for machine-shops and manufactories of various kinds, such as—Clothing manufactories, Saw Mills, etc., and also for agricultural purposes; Therefore, the Municipality, considering:

1st. That the territory of the Republic of Honduras offers a home to all foreigners, particularly to the industrious who may wish to settle upon its soil;

2d. That Mr. Green Malcolm, for himself and in the name of his fellow settlers, offers to establish machines and manufactories in the country, and to teach to the natives of the soil the use and management of the same, and other trades;

3d. To establish a highway for transit by the Chamlicon, between Omoa and San Pedro, to import and export merchandise for themselves and for the natives, requiring from the latter such reasonable prices [for transport] as will amount to about one-third the hire of a mule. ["*cobrandoles a estos precios equitativitos, tanto, que les cueste dos or tres veces menos que el alquiler de un mula por el transporte*"—receiving from the latter fair prices such that it will cost them two or three times less than the rental of a mule for transport.]

4. To live in good harmony with the natives, fraternizing with and helping each other.

5. To respect the authorities, the laws and the religion of the country, and to contribute on their part, to the respect, observance and execution of the same, so that if any of them should fail in this particular, they shall demand and see that he be punished according to the laws.

6. To establish colleges ["*colegios*"—secondary schools] and schools for their children and those of the natives.

And the municipality, after hearing the Council did therefore resolve:—

1. To grant to each and every foreigner wishing to settle in San Pedro, the right to build on the public lands of this community, houses of residence, machine-shops and manufactories of various kinds, for cloths and clothing, saw mills, and such others as Cotton, Sugar Cane, Coffee, &c.

2. That the North Americans who have arrived or may hereafter arrive here for the purpose of settling in San Pedro, shall not oppose any Central-American, or citizens of any friendly nations who may come to settle, and erect buildings on the unoccupied lands in their vicinity.

3. That their right in relation to public lands shall be the same as those enjoyed by the citizens of San Pedro, for cultivation, for making lumber, whether for building purposes or for the use of their establishments, or other purposes, excepting for exportation as an article of merchandise.

4. They shall have an equal right to the medicinal plants and wild fruits on the public lands; also the right to cut wood for fuel, and to the use of the water for their machines, whenever they may need them, provided no prejudice result therefrom to the public at large.

5. That no citizen of San Pedro shall molest or disturb them in the possession of whatever they may acquire under this Act; and any one so doing, shall be punished as a disturber of the peace and tranquility of the community.

6. That this Act be communicated to Mr. Malcolm, that he may present it to His Excellency the President of the Republic, in order that, should he deem it expedient, he may give it his sovereign approval, or otherwise dispose as he may think proper.

Thus agreed, and signed by the Municipality, the Council and citizens who concurred, before me, the present Secretary, to which I hereby certify.—Monico Pedilla, by the Señor Regidor Don Pablo Cadiz, who cannot sign his name, and by me as Syndic, Antonio Zarabia; for the Councilmen Don Juan Zuniga, Don Juan Cadiz, and Don Luis Matamoros, who cannot write, and for myself Manuel Cruz. Timoteo Quintero, Lazaro Bardalis. Por mi padre [for my father], Seraphio Reyes, who cannot sign, and for Messrs. Jorge Vallecillo and Concepcion Vallecillo,—Andres Reyes. Manuel Cadiz, José Reynaud—Rufino Gonzalez—Eduardo Buckmar. Jose Maria Merlo, Secretario: This agrees with the original from which I copied it literally, at the verbal request of Mr. Malcolm, in San Pedro, on the 23d day of the month of April, 1867,—José Maria Merlo, Secretary.

Document 4.

On the third of May, 1867, the communication below was forwarded to the authorities.

To his Excellency the President and Executive officers of the Republic of Honduras;

GENTLEMEN:

The undersigned respectfully submits to your consideration, that on the 10th of April, after a passage of ten days, I arrived in the city of Omoa with seventy souls, emigrants to your beautiful land. These persons consist of men, women and children, who are what might be termed the forerunners of perhaps thousands of the best citizens of the Southern States, of the United States. We wish to make this our home. To find in this that which we have lost in our own native land, liberty. To make this what our country was before it was destroyed by our enemies. Our desire is to become citizens of the Republic at once, to be a part of your people, to claim your protection, to defend you with our lives from foreign invasion, and to do our whole duty to our adopted country. In coming among you we would state that on account of our recent great misfortunes, many of us are greatly impoverished, and without going into further preliminary remarks, would give this as our reason for asking you to grant the following privileges and donations.

1st. A grant of land as indicated in the accompanying map.

2d. A free port at Port Acabellos for three years, for the exclusive benefit of the colony.

3d. The exclusive navigation of the rivers Chamilicon, Ulua and their tributries [*sic*] for ten years.

4th. The right to build roads through public and private lands, for the benefit of the Colony and Government.

5th. The right to construct aqueducts and bring water through our and adjacent lands.

6th. The exemption from taxation for two years from the day of arrival.

7th. The privilege of enacting our own municipal regulations in conformity with the laws of the Republic.

8th. The privilege of organizing our city adjacent to San Pedro, separately from that town and naming it the city of Medina.

9th. The exclusive privilege of establishing manufactories for the manufacture of woolen and cotton goods in the Republic for ten years.

10th. The exclusive privilege of introducing for five years, wagons, buggies and carriages, the common sense sewing machine, washing machines of all descriptions with machines for making tin-ware.

11th. The privilege of distilling liquors from the productions of our farms. The privilege of planting and harvesting all seeds in our colony, and introducting [sic] the still known as the "Log still."

12th. The privilege of introducing for eight years the circular saw mill run by steam or water, planing machines and shingle machines. The above we acknowledge appears liberal and we should not have you think us asking too much, for we by these privileges and grants, desire and are determined as far as possible to use them to the improvement, development, and welfare of the country was well as ourselves.

With the highest consideration,

I am gentlemen, your obedient servant.

(Signed) G. MALCOLM

Comayagua, Honduras, C.A., May 3, 1867

Document 5.

To which the following was returned.

The President, in whom resides the supreme executive power of the Republic of Honduras.

Whereas, Mr. Green Malcolm, a native of the United States, for himself and in behalf of various families of his nationality has presented a petition, soliciting permission to settle in the territory of the Republic, with the privileges of citizens of Honduras, and subjecting themselves to the laws now in force or that may hereafter be enacted in the country, with which intent they ask certain privileges and concessions.

CONSIDERING

That the Republic is in need of industrious Immigrants to develop the natural resources which abound in our country, and that the Legislative Decree of 23rd February of last year authorizes the Government to protect this class of enterprises;

Therefore, now makes and decrees the following concessions;

1st. It is permitted to the honest and industrious Immigrants from the United States, of the South of North America, who have already come or may hereafter come to this country, to establish, in the District of San Pedro, Department of Santa Barbara, a cummunity [sic] which shall bear the title of the City of Medina.

2d. Besides the common use which, the Municipality of San Pedro has granted to said Immigrants in its public lands, under the conditions laid down in the Act presented by Mjr. Malcolm, and which the Government has approved, they are also granted the national lands contiguous to those of San Pedro towards the south, and included within the following boundaries; the Chamlicon and the base of the mountains of the south-west of the said village of San Pedro, a delineation of which will be opportunely made.

3. Port Cortés shall be free during three years, in order that the settlers of the city of Medina may introduce everything necessary for their consumption, and for the establishment of houses, manufactories, machinery, etc.

4. Navigation by steam or horse power of the rivers Chamlicon, Ulua and its tributaries, shall be the exclusive privilege of said Immigrants for a period of eight years.

5th. They are also granted the following exclusive privileges:
1st. For ten years, the establishment of machines for manufacturing cotton, woolen and other fibrous goods, and for refining sugar.
2d. For eight years, the establishment of steam or water power mills, for sawing and planing lumber, also wash machines ["*y hacer tejamani*"—and to make shingles].
3d. The introduction during five years, of wagons, buggies, carriages, the sewing machine known as the "Common Sense Sewing Machine," the machine for making tin-ware and still known as the "Log Still," for the distillation of spirituous liquors, and the sale of the same, under the regulations relative to this branch.

6. They shall have the right of constructing roads over national lands, or lands of private persons, for the benefit of themselves and of the Government, and to construct aqueducts to conduct water for the irrigation of their lands.

7. The settlers of the city of Medina, shall be exempt from military service and forced contributions during two years from their arrival.

8. They shall have the right to elect for their government, and in conformity with the laws of the Republic, a municipal body; and may, in the meantime, and until they number 500 persons, be ruled by a Governor and a Judge of the Peace whom they shall elect from among themselves, those officers being subordinate, the former to the Governor of Santa Barbara, and the latter to the "Judge in the First Instance" of Omoa.

9th. They shall have the right to make their own rules and regulations for the internal government of the cummunity [*sic*], in conformity with the laws of the Republic, and shall submit these to the approbation of the Congress, or the Supreme Executive Power.

10. The articles which said settlers may ship in the ports of the Republic shall be free from all export duty during a period of eight years.

These concessions shall in no manner operate to the prejudice of the projected Inter-Oceanic Railroad; for, whatever privileges have been, or may hereafter be granted to the latter, shall be an exception to the present concessions.

Let it be understood: that the privileges before mentioned relative to the establishment of machines, shall be confined to the departments of Santa Barbara, Gracies and Comayagua; exception for the machine for manufacturing cloths, which shall extend to the whole Republic.

If within three years the number of persons in the city now to be founded does not ascend to five hundred at least, the privileges granted under this Act shall remain without effect; but, in such case the immigrants who may already be established shall have the right of property to such portions of the land granted as shall be found under cultivation.

Written in Comayagua, in the Government House, on the 8th day of May, 1867—J. Lopez, Ponseano Leiva.

{SEAL}   A true copy,
     San Pedro, Jan. 29th, 1868
     J. REYNAUD

Document 6.

In May, 1867, Major Malcolm was made Inspector of Foreign Immigration, the following being a copy of his commission from the Government.

Comayagua, May 8, 1867

Mr. Green Malcolm.

Sir:

The government, considering that you have already been admitted as a citizen of this Republic, and satisfied of your abilities and good wishes for the prosperity of the country, has deemed it expedient to nominate you by a resolution passed this day, Inspector of Foreign Immigration for the coast and the interior of the Department of Santa Barbara, making it your duty to report to the Government, whatever measures you may adopt, in your official capacity, to remove all difficulties that may arise and to promote the views of Government on the subject of immigration.

Hoping that you will accept this nomination, I have the pleasure to subscribe myself yours respectfully,

PONCIANO LEIVA

Given under the seal of the Ministry of Interior Relations and Government.

Document 7.

The Council [of Medina] elected in 1867 continued in office till the 18th of February, 1868, when a new Council was elected, the following gentlemen being chosen; Dr. G. P. Frierson the Presiding Officer.

In consequence of a difference of opinion existing between the authorities of San Pedro and Maj. Malcolm concerning the Mayor's [Major's?] authority over, and right to grant titles to the town lands as Agent of the Bureau of Emigration, the matter was put to rest by the Major signing the following paper, which was a matter of public record.

Dr. G. P. Frierson	L. G. Pirkle
D. P. Ferguson	G. A. Haralson
W. B. Tingle, Sr.	A. J. Hill, Secry.

(Copy.)

"As I do not wish to be misunderstood or misrepresented, I hereby repeat what I have stated to Dr. Frierson and others at different times, that any one desiring to settle on the District of land called Medina, and which was conceded by the town of San Pedro in an official Act dated April 22, 1867, to settlers, have the ability, with my consent, to choose their location and 150 acres to a man of family and 100 acres to a single man, and that they have the right to apply to the authorities of San Pedro for titles or rely upon my obtaining titles for them as they may choose. That I make no objection to any settler except on account of unworthiness to be established by me. The cost to be at the expense of each settler, unless the General Government decide that titles are only to be made by the authorities of San Pedro; and in that case, I obligate myself to refund all such costs made to me. In the event that the General Government decide that titles to said lands shall be made through other channels, then I obligate myself to furnish indisputable titles, without additional costs, and in whatever manner the Government may direct. Having promised as a citizen of the country and as an officer of Government, to be controlled in all things by my superiors.

February 24, 1868

G. Malcolm

(Signed)

Witnesses:

(Signed) G. P. Frierson,

W. J. Walters,

L. G. Pirkle.

Document 8.

The following notice being found posted, is copied for information.

NOTICE

At a meeting of the City Council of Medina, February 24, the following resolution was passed:

That any one wishing a lot in Medina, can obtain the same by paying register fee, (one dollar) with the privilege of buying an additional lot for the sum of 25 dollars; provided the first lot be cleared immediately and improved within six months; the second to be cleared and improved within twelve months. A house to be erected on one of the lots within six months. The above privilege to close on June first.

February 26, 1868
G. P. Frierson
Chairman

Facts, Figures, and Travel Tips

✳

BRITISH HONDURAS

LAWS.

Concerning the laws, it is hardly worth saying anything, as they are *English*. Suffice it to say, that, here law prevails, and this is one of the most orderly communities we have ever visited.

LANDS.

Those who have followed us this far will be able to form a pretty correct idea of the soil, and its location, and only a few words are necessary on this point. The idea prevails that there is very little thin land, which is not the case, as we not unfrequently found clay at a depth of eight inches, and much land containing too large a proportion of sand. The cahoon palm, which is received as a sure indication of rich land was found growing on soil both wet and dry, rich and poor. That there is high land in British Honduras cannot be questioned, but it is not on the coast, anywhere south of Belize that was visited by us, except at "All Pines" and "Seven Hills," and we were informed the best lands could be found in that part of the colony. We examined the lands on the rivers; and as far as examined, they are generally flat, and present every indication of being subject to overflow. We found high ground on the Middle River and Golden-stream, and have no doubt there is a ridge of land between all these rivers that is above overflow, but what is its extent, and what is the character of the country between those points and the rivers, or the coasts?

RIVERS.

The rivers of the colony examined by us are truly beautiful streams, almost entirely without obstructions, and generally very deep. The Golden-stream, Rio-Grande, and Moho might be navigated for twenty miles at least, by the Mississippi River steamer General Quitman, when once over the bar, and at high tide should have no difficulty in passing that point.

REPTILES AND INSECTS.

During our stay in British Honduras, we saw but two snakes one of which was killed by Dr. F. on the Golden-stream, and the other we saw at All Pines; the first being unknown to us, and the second a garter snake. Mosquitoes, sand flies and bottle flies, except when the sea breeze prevails are very numerous and annoying. The first is an old enemy, and the second not unknown in this country, but the third belongs to a different latitude—we will describe it. In size it is almost the same as the turkey gnat, and punctures the flesh, usually without causing pain, leaving as its mark a small red spot of blood drawn to the outer layer of the skin. For eighteen or twenty-four hours this does not annoy, but at about that time an itching sensation is produced, and you scratch continually, when the hands swell considerably, presenting a very unnatural appearance. We were fortunately told to puncture those spots as soon as discovered, press out the blood and bathe with salt water, which was done, and no unpleasant results followed their bite. We have seen hundreds of these bites on the hands of a single individual. Ants are very numerous and destructive to gardens. House-flies, so familiar to us, are here almost unknown.

FRUITS.

The orange, lemon, lime, plantain, banana, guava, pine-apple, cocoa-nut, and we might add all the fruits of the tropics, *in their season.*

VEGETABLES.

Much the same as with us, and in addition the yam, yampa, casava, coco or malanga, and others of less importance. The yam is very much like our sweet potato in appearance, and grows to a large size, frequently weighing ten or fifteen pounds; and when boiled, very closely resembles the Irish potato. The yampa is also a root, but does not attain the size of the yam, and is in taste a medium between the Irish and sweet potato. The casava and malanga are also roots, the first of which grows to the weight of four or five pounds and has already been described, and the second to the size of our Irish potato, and is the nearest approach to that vegetable of all we have named.

CEREALS.

Corn is grown, and according to report, two crops are raised in one year. We were shown some of this grain at Seven Hills the ears being of medium size and full to the ends. It is very farinaceous and is early attacked by weevil, that in a short time leave nothing but husk. Many persons claimed that not only two crops a year can be raised, but sixty bushels an acre to the crop. We saw nothing that promised a larger return than fifteen bushels but we did not measure either land or corn.

Of rice we saw some that was very fine. Two crops a year are also claimed for this. We are satisfied this is a very fine country for its production, and that the yield will be both large in quantity and excellent in quality.

THEABROMA CACAO.

This tree, from the fruit of which the chocolate of commerce is made, we did not see growing in British Honduras, but *heard of one* south of Belize, and of a patch of twenty or more on the Belize River. Parties who have tried it say they did not succeed well with it.

COFFEE.

Did not see a tree growing in the colony. A gentleman of my acquaintance said he did not believe there was a tree in British Honduras, but was told there was *one at Corosal.* We know of no reason why both coffee and cacao will not grow here equally as well as in Spanish Honduras, and believed if proper locations are selected and the necessary care and attention are bestowed they will succeed.

DOMESTIC ANIMALS.

Of horses, mules, cattle, hogs and sheep, there are very few in the country; Spanish Honduras and Guatemala being dependent on as the sources of supply.

GOVERNMENT OFFICERS.

His Excellency, Lt. Gov. Jas. Robt. Longdon. Private Secretary, Fredk. Harcourt Hamblin. Col. Secry., Controller of Customs, and clerk to the Council, Lt. P. J. Hankin, R. N. Col. Secretary, Austin Wm. Cox. Col. Treasurer, Antonio Mathé. Attorney general, Joseph H. Phillips. Bishop, Bishop of Kingston. Chief Justice, Hon. R. J. Corner. Crown Surveyor, J. H. Faber.

Immigration Agent, A. W. Cox, and many others; the above being the most important. The Legislature is composed of the Lt. Governor and a Legislative Assembly of twenty-one members, viz., eighteen elective and three nominated by the Crown, also an Executive Council of six members.

Executive Council, (styled honorable,) Officer Com. troops, Col. Secretary, Treasurer, Attorney-General *Ex Officio:* A. W. Cox, A. Mathé, P. Toledo.

Imports of the colony for 1866 . . . . £169,033 08
Export 277,155 16

American Consul . . . . A. C. Prindle
Spanish Honduras . . . . J. E. Mutrie

Census Population of colony, April 7, 1861. 25,635
Present .. .. Belize about. 6,000

The population of the colony, including the towns, is almost entirely colored.

DUES.

On the effects of agricultural immigrants there is no duty; but such persons on their way to Spanish Honduras will be required to pay "Transshipment dues," varying from twenty-five to fifty cents per package; the latter to be paid for each barrel of flour and pork.

Many being under the impression that "living" is cheaper at Belize than in the United States, the following from the "Belize Honduras Colonist" of February 29th, 1868, will enable them to form a better idea perhaps than they at present have of the subject. Gold or silver to be used in payment.

FINANCIAL AND COMMERCIAL
Rate of Exchange of Bills on England is $500 per £100 sterling.

Flour	$14 to 15 per bbl.
Rice	$5 to 6 " 100 lbs.
Corn	$1 to 1.12½ per bbl.
Plantains	26½ to 75c " 100
Beef	$18 to 25 per bbl.
Butter	44 to 50c " bbl.
Lard	14 to 16c " "
Pork, Prime	$24 per bbl.

" Mess	$24 to 25 per bbl.
Fish	$6 to 7 per 100 lbs.
Fowls	$4.50 to 6 " doz.
Sugar, brown	$7 to 7½ " 100 lbs.
" white	$16 to 19 " "
" loaf	$18 to 21 " "
Coffee	18 to 20 " "
Tea	$1.25 to 1.50 per lb.
Tobacco, leaf	25 to 32 " 100 lbs.
Cedar	25 to $40 " M. ft.
Pitch Pine Lumber	35 to $40 " "
White Pine	40 to $45 " "
Mahogany boards	$80 " "

SPANISH HONDURAS
OR
THE REPUBLIC OF HONDURAS

The productions of both Spanish Honduras and British Honduras are very much the same with the exception of cacao and coffee, both of which seem to us better here than in British Honduras. Mahogany, fustic, log-wood, rose-wood, and other woods of value are alike common in both countries, as is also the caoutchouc, or India-rubber. Most of the wood of both Spanish Honduras and British Honduras will not split, and the fencing is usually made of logs, or the "Pimento." The following we were told would split, though we saw no rails in the country. Cedar, one kind of mahogany, laurel, jabon, pine, (which grows on the mountains) and one kind of oak (we saw only the live oak.) Much of the timber is liable to be attacked by worms and is unsuited to building purposes. The following being used for houses; cedar, mahogany, black laurel, frijoea, oak cabrahatcha, and the mother of cacao; the last being very fine for posts, as it is said to be as durable as our locust. The *Motaté*, a hedge plant, is used very extensively, (which we do not remember to have mentioned) which grows to the height of six to eight feet, and resembles the tuft which grows on the top of the pine apple, with briers on each edge, and is impenetrable.

FRUITS.

It is a mistaken idea that fruits of most kinds can be had at all seasons of the year, and that they are superior to the same kinds imported into the United States. The banana and plantain are always to be had, as is also the orange, in some sections, but they *are not* superior in flavor to the same fruits, imported, as it is necessary to gather them, except the orange, in an unripe state, even here, to prevent their destruction by birds. The pine apple is perhaps superior in flavor when left to ripen on the plant, that being the opinion expressed by many, though we could discover but little, if any difference. There are no peaches no pears, no apples and we hardly think any one would exchange those fruits for all that are raised in Honduras. There are two fibrous plants that are worthy of mention, which are extensively used by the natives though comparatively little is prepared for export. The *"Pete,"* or silk grass; and the *"Mascal."* From the first fish lines and hammocks are made, and from the second, cordage. The fibre is almost precisely like the manilla, being equally strong, and is prepared without "water rotting." These plants so closely resemble the *"Motaté"* in appearance that they are often mistaken for it.

GAME.

In British Honduras but little game was seen, but in Spanish Honduras can be found the deer, turkey, a species of grouse, and the *"Qualm"* which is a bird not unlike the pea fowl, but a little smaller; also rabbits, quails, and pigeons.

FISH.

While the waters of the sea furnish fish in abundance and in great variety, they were not found to be plentiful in the streams in either country we visited.

DUTIES.

The Import duty is 40 percent on all things but liquor, that being 30 per cent; 10 percent of the 40 per cent has to be paid in coin, and 30 per cent in Government paper, which reduces it to about 15 percent in coin. On liquor, 20 per cent has to be paid in coin, and the balance in Government paper.

EXPORTS AND IMPORTS.

The annual exports are about as follows: Imports being about the same as exports in amount.

Exports.—Mahogany, and other woods		$300,000
"	Bullion	250,000
"	Cattle	150,000
"	Indigo, sugar, hides, tobacco and Sarsaparilla	250,000
	Total	$950,000

REVENUES.

The revenues of the country amount to about $300,000, a large portion of which is derived from the sale of *Aguardiente,* (native rum) and tobacco, both of which are Government monopolies.

Most of the money in circulation is the *Macaco* or cut money, though there is now considerable American coin to be seen, which passes for its full value, except the dime and half dime.

The government is popular and representative and composed of three distinct powers, viz: Legislative, Executive, and Judicial. The first residing in the General Assembly, the second in the President, and the third in the Courts.

The religion is the *Roman Catholic to the exclusion of all others.* The following being an extract from the Constitution of the country on that subject.

Capitulo 3°
DEL GOBIERNO Y DE LA RELIGION
Art. 7°—El gobierno de la Republica es popular representativo; y se ejercera por tres Poderes distintos: Legislativo, Ejecutivo y Judicial.

Art 8°—La Religion de la Republica es la Cristiana, Catholica, Apostolica Roman, con exclusion del ejercicio publico de cualquiera otra. El Gobierno la protege; pero ni este ni autoridad alguna tendran intervencion en el ejercicio privado de las otras que se establezcan en el pais, si estas no tienden a deprimir la dominante y a alterar el orden publico.

Persons born in the state, or any state of Central America are recognized as citizens. Foreigners may acquire the right by act of the Legislature, but as soon as they declare their intention to become citizens are entitled to the protection of citizens.

All citizens over the age of 21 are entitled to vote, but after the year 1870 only those who can read and write will be entitled to that privilege. Any one convicted of a crime is deprived the right of suffrage. Foreigners become naturalized by marrying in the state, or by holding a given amount of property.

LABORERS AND SERVANTS.

The price usually paid for men, field hands, is from five to seven dollars per month and their provision, and from eight to ten when they feed themselves. For a cook woman, $3.00 per month. For washing (family of four) $2.00 a month—washing not done on the premises; for a girl 12 years of age, from $1.00 to $1.50 per month; and for boys of the same age $3.00 per month. As is the case in British Honduras, laborers and servants *are scarce*, and the few to be found are seldom anxious to hire. We do not know of a family of immigrants at San Pedro provided with native servants, they doing their work in most cases themselves; though there may be some.

DOMESTIC ARRANGEMENTS.

We have said there is not a chimney at San Pedro; this is the case also in British Honduras except in the towns. The contrivance for cooking is a platform raised about two feet, on which clay to the depth of six inches is placed, and at one side, or rather edge, several little horse-shoe or semicircular fire places are made on which to place the cooking vessels. It is astonishing to see how small a quantity of wood is necessary to cook a meal by this arrangement. A lady who has lived here for several years informed me she preferred these fire places to a cook stove. Such a thing as a bucket is not to be seen; porous earthen jars being used instead, the constant evaporation from the surface of which reduces the temperature of the water several degrees. On the table, earthen bottles of a similar material are used instead of pitchers. The women are the most superior washers, yet a wash tub is not used but what is called a *Battea*, which is a tray, varying is size, but usually two feet and a half in length by one and a half in width. For the benefit of bachelors we will state that they have no use for a wash board, and that only thirty-seven and a half cents per dozen is charged for washing when soap is furnished them, and one dollar if the clothes are starched and ironed. Their work in this line ought to be well done, for our experience (before we commenced doing our own washing) proved that they required one day to wash, one to dry, one to iron, and from one to two more to bring it home, whether it was one piece or a dozen. It seems almost impossible for one person to do anything where two can be employed. In milking, one holds the calabash while another milks with both hands; the calf being tied to a foreleg of the cow.

DOMESTIC ANIMALS.

Neat cattle are plentiful, and can be bought for, from 5 to 19 dollars each, a short distance from San Pedro. Horses and mules are abundant, but very small, and vary in price from 15 to 50 dollars, the latter price being paid for such animals as can be bought with us for the same sum in different funds. The hogs are *very fine* and can be bought low; pork selling for 3 cents per pound. This is no country for sheep, but the goat seems to do very well.

REPTILES AND INSECTS.

We did not see, during our stay in Spanish Honduras, a single snake—though they are said to be numerous. There are some bottle-flies, but not so many as in British Honduras, and in certain localities sand flies are very numerous and annoying. While we saw no mosquitoes at San Pedro, if it is desired to see them in their most gigantic proportions, take a trip on the Chemlicon. During our stay on that river they proved themselves to be the largest, strongest, and most persistent in their efforts to annoy, carried the sharpest weapon, and used it more vigorously than any it had ever before been our misfortune to encounter. Ants are both very large and numerous, and those who succeed in establishing a kitchen garden, and in enjoying the fruit of their labor thus bestowed, consider themselves very fortunate.

OUTFIT FOR HONDURAS.

Having found that we made more than one mistake in this respect, will state that our linen clothing was found not suited to the climate, as we were frequently uncomfortably cool, and it would have been better if thin woolen material had been selected instead. We were induced to purchase "moccasins" at Belize, and found them to be of little service, though they are worn by men engaged in cutting for export the woods of the country, and by a very large proportion of the natives. If we had provided ourselves with a pair of good boots, it would have been much better. We also found that cotton socks did not answer a good purpose, and it would have been better had we been provided with those made of wool. It is best to have all articles that are to be carried to San Pedro, in packages of one hundred pounds, when it can be done, as two hundred pounds is a load for a mule.

MONEY.

American silver coins, with the exception of dimes and half dimes, pass in both British Honduras and Spanish Honduras, for their full value, and in British Honduras 2½ per cent is allowed for American Gold coin in making purchases, in conformity to law of the country, though it can frequently be sold for 3 or 4 per cent. The English shilling will pass for as much as an American quarter, which fact having been ascertained by us before we left New Orleans, an ample supply of that coin was provided.

Notes

PART I

1. Throughout the text, we refer to the British colony as British Honduras rather than by its modern national name of Belize in order not to confuse the colony with the city. At the same time, we reserve the name Honduras for the Republic of Honduras, which Swett frequently calls Spanish Honduras.

2. For example, see former General P. T. Beauregard's letter in the *Vicksburg Daily Herald*, December 23, 1865, in which he states that despite an initial interest in emigrating to Brazil, President Andrew Johnson's "generous sentiments" toward the South persuaded him to stay in the U.S. South.

3. Daniel E. Sutherland, *The Confederate Carpetbaggers* (Baton Rouge: Louisiana State University Press, 1988).

4. Gaines M. Foster, *Ghosts of the Confederacy: Defeat, the Lost Cause, and the Emergence of the New South, 1865 to 1913* (New York: Oxford University Press, 1987), 16–17.

5. It is clear that some people did head south as individuals. For example, see David P. Werlich, *Admiral of the Amazon: John Randolph Tucker, His Confederate Colleagues, and Peru* (Charlottesville: University of Virginia Press, 1990), about a former Confederate naval officer who became "Admiral of the [Peruvian] Amazon." Daniel E. Sutherland, "Exiles, Emigrants, and Sojourners: The Post-Civil War Confederate Exodus in Perspective," *Civil War History* 31 (1985): 237–256, is a useful discussion of the reasons why so many Southerners desired to leave the South immediately after the war.

6. Michael Wayne, *The Reshaping of Plantation Society: The Natchez District, 1860–1880* (Baton Rouge: Louisiana State University Press, 1983), 2–10.

7. Nancy D. Bercaw, *Gendered Freedoms: Race, Rights, and the Politics of Household in the Delta, 1861–1875* (Gainesville: University Press of Florida, 2003), 7–13.

8. For the influence of the Whig Party, see James T. Currie, *Enclave: Vicksburg and Her Plantations, 1863–1870* (Jackson: University of Mississippi Press, 1980), xvii, 186–187, 203; Christopher Charles Morris, *Becoming Southern: The Evolution of a Way of Life, Warren County and Vicksburg, Mississippi, 1770–1860* (New York: Oxford University Press, 1995), 129–131, 144–147.

9. Several sources maintain that Charles Swett was a graduate of West Point and that at beginning of the Civil War, he resigned his commission in the U.S. Army to join the

Confederate army. Nevertheless, *The Register of Graduates and Former Cadets, United States Military Academy* (2002 bicentennial edition), has no record of Charles Swett attending the U.S. Military Academy at West Point. In addition, neither Thomas Holdup Stevens Hamersly, comp. and ed., *Complete Regular Army Register of the United States, for One Hundred Years (1779 to 1879)* (Washington, D.C.: T. H. S. Hamersly, 1880), nor Francis B. Heitman, *Historical Register and Dictionary of the United States Army, from Its Organization, September 29, 1789, to March 2, 1903* (Washington, D.C.: Government Printing Office, 1903; repr., Baltimore: Genealogical Publishing, 1994), lists him as a member of the U.S. Army. Given Swett's family's economic status, he probably at least graduated from a young man's academy.

10. Dunbar Rowland mistakenly identifies Charles Swett as one of the Warren County delegates; see his *A History of Mississippi: Heart of the South*, vol. 1 (Chicago and Jackson, Miss.: S. J. Clarke, 1925), 781.

11. One issue that Marshall and Brooke agreed on was to continue the ban on the African slave trade. J. L. Power (Convention Reporter), *Proceedings of the Mississippi State Convention, Held January 7th to 26th, A.D. 1861. Including the Ordinances, as Finally Adopted, Important Speeches, and a List of Members, Showing the Postoffice, Profession, Nativity, Politics, Age, Religious Pre[ference]* (Jackson, Miss.: Power & Cadwallader, Book and Job Printers, 1861), 12–14, 38–39.

12. James L. Roark, *Masters without Slaves: Southern Planters in the Civil War and Reconstruction* (New York: W. W. Norton, 1977), 2–9. For an example of the fear of seceding, John W. Wood, in his *Union and Secession in Mississippi* (Memphis, Tenn.: Sanders, Parrish & Whitmore, 1863), declared himself proud to be a slaveholder from a long line of slaveholders but believed secession to be such a serious mistake that in the pamphlet's subtitle he identifies himself as "the Union member of the Mississippi State Convention who refused to sign the ordinance of secession, or to commit himself in any way to the secession movement." See Dunbar Rowland, *A History of Mississippi: Heart of the South*, vol. 2 (Chicago and Jackson, Miss.: S. J. Clarke, 1925), 111, for the vote.

13. This paragraph and the following three are drawn from Charles Swett, "A Brief Narrative of Warren Lt. Artillery, Known during 'Civil War,' 1861, '62, '63, '64 & '65, as Swett's Battery, Hardee's Confs, 'Army of Northern Ky.' and 'Army of Tenn,'" (1908), typewritten manuscript available in the Old Court House Museum, Vicksburg, Miss. Memoirs written by veterans of the Civil War were commonplace by the 1880s, and Swett did not respond to his family's entreaties to record his own until 1908. It is written in a style similar to that of the 1868 pamphlet—a detached tone describing what happened and who was there, and emphasizing the logistics and terrain of various battles. Each of these is followed by an account of those who died or were wounded. The issue of slavery is not mentioned.

14. U.S. War Department, *The War of the Rebellion: A Compilation of the Official Records of the Union and Confederate Armies* (Washington, D.C.: Government Printing Office), Series I, vol. 10, Part I (1884), 574; vol. 16, Part I (1886), 1131–1132; vol. 23, Part I (1889), 601; vol. 30, Part II (1890), 159, 255–257, 750; vol. 32, Part III (1891), 690, 693. For a summary of Swett's Battery's activities, see Swett, "Brief Narrative of Warren Lt. Artillery"; Dunbar Rowland, *Military History of Mississippi, 1803–1898* (Spartanburg, S.C.: Reprint Co., 1978), 494–498; and Charles Swett, "Report of Captain Charles Swett, Acting Chief of Artillery (1863)," in *The Rebellion Record, a Diary of American Events*, vol. 10 (New York: D. Van Nostrand, 1867), 478–479. In 1974 the governor of Mississippi

reactivated Swett's Battery "To commemorate this battery." http://mdah.state.ms.us/manuscripts/z1363.html, accessed September 12, 2008.

15. The quotations from the memoir are in Swett, "Brief Narrative of Warren Lt. Artillery," 16, 17.

16. One indication of the importance of Vicksburg is the quantity and quality of the scholarship devoted to it. Morris, *Becoming Southern*; Christopher Waldrep, *Vicksburg's Long Shadow: The Civil War Legacy of Race and Remembrance* (Lanham, Md.: Rowman & Littlefield, 2005); and Currie, *Enclave*, are good social and political histories that complement each other. Peter Franklin Walker, *Vicksburg: A People at War, 1860–1865* (Chapel Hill: University of North Carolina Press, 1960), and Samuel Carter, *The Final Fortress: The Campaign for Vicksburg, 1862–1863* (New York: St. Martin's Press, 1980), focus on the city's war years.

17. For an informative account of the siege of Vicksburg from a white woman's perspective, see Emilie Riley McKinley, *From the Pen of a She-Rebel: The Civil War Diary of Emilie Riley McKinley*, ed. Gordon A. Cotton (Columbia: University of South Carolina Press, 2001).

18. Currie, *Enclave*, 5–7; Waldrep, *Vicksburg's Long Shadow*, 174.

19. Currie, *Enclave*, xiv, 211; Waldrep, *Vicksburg's Long Shadow*, 66.

20. Waldrep, *Vicksburg's Long Shadow*, 245–248, 283.

21. U.S. Bureau of the Census, *Historical Statistics of the United States, Colonial Times to 1970*, Part 1 (Washington, D.C.: Government Printing Office, 1975), 24–36.

22. While Mississippi did make slavery illegal by changing its state constitution in 1865, it did not ratify the Thirteenth Amendment until 1995.

23. For examples of Marshall and Swett becoming members of smaller minorities, see *Journal of the Proceedings and Debates in the Constitutional Convention of the State of Mississippi, August 1865* (Jackson, Miss.: E. M. Yerger, State Printer, 1865), 54, 71, 281. In the order listed, they were in the minorities of votes that passed 61 to 33, 63 to 28, and 87 to 11.

24. Quoted in Rowland, *History of Mississippi*, vol. 2, 111. This proposal might have been modeled on New York's property qualification for registering and voting. New York had no property qualification for whites but required $250 of real property "above all debts and encumbrances" for African Americans. Alexander Keyssar, *The Right to Vote: The Contested History of Democracy in the United States* (New York: Basic Books, 2000), 332.

25. For the colonization proposal to send freedmen to foreign or "empty" national lands, see *Journal of the Proceedings and Debates in the Constitutional Convention of the State Of Mississippi*, 247. For an example of antisecessionist eloquence that questioned slavery, see the remarks by William Yerger, a lawyer representing Hinds County, in *Journal of the Proceedings and Debates in the Constitutional Convention of the State Of Mississippi*, 151–164. Rowland, *History of Mississippi*, vol. 2, 105–115, notes the absence of discussions of race.

26. The letters appear in the *Vicksburg Daily Herald*, April 3, 1867. They are followed by a news item on the same page reporting that one of the principals in the original quarrel had challenged one of the mediators to a duel, and mediation had failed.

27. Dan T. Carter, *When the War Was Over: The Failure of Self-Reconstruction in the South, 1865–1867* (Baton Rouge: Louisiana State University Press, 1985); Keyssar, *Right to Vote*, 87–93. The *Vicksburg Daily Herald*, October, 26, 28, and 29, 1865, expresses optimism of a very short period of Reconstruction, and editorials of January 5, 1867, and

April 3, 1867, praised Andrew Johnson's opposition to the U.S. Congress's changes in Reconstruction.

28. Carpetbaggers were defined by white Southerners as Northerners who had moved to the South after the war to pursue economic and political opportunities or to teach and "missionize" black Southerners. Scalawags were defined as white Southerners who worked with the Republicans in reconstruction. Many had opposed secession and the war. Southern whites used both labels as pejoratives.

29. Ironically, Revels supported amnesty for ex-Confederates and the restoration of their citizenship. He served in the Senate for one year and was succeeded by James L. Alcorn, a former Confederate who became a "scalawag" and joined the Republican Party. Philip Dray, *Capitol Men: The Epic Story of Reconstruction through the Lives of the First Black Congressmen* (Boston: Houghton Mifflin, 2008), describes Revels's political career in the context of his African American colleagues.

30. Mary Elizabeth Massey, *Refugee Life in the Confederacy* (Baton Rouge: Louisiana State University Press, 1964), 35–41; Roark, *Masters without Slaves*, 83–85; Paul D. Escott, *After Secession: Jefferson Davis and the Failure of Confederate Nationalism* (Baton Rouge: Louisiana State University Press, 1978), 109–112.

31. U.S. Bureau of the Census, *Population Schedules of the Eighth Census of the United States, Mississippi* (Washington, D.C.: National Archives Microfilm Publications), Roll 592, 106 (Warren County, 1860); U.S. Bureau of the Census, *Population Schedules of the Ninth Census of the United States, Mississippi* (Washington, D.C.: National Archives Microfilm Publications), Roll 235, 27 (Copiah County, 1870).

32. The Thirteenth Amendment, ratified in 1865, also freed without compensation the 500,000 slaves in the slave states that did not secede, although Maryland abolished slavery before the amendment went into effect. Donald B. Dodd and Wynelle S. Dodd, *Historical Statistics of the South, 1790–1970* (University: University of Alabama Press, 1973), 2–65; U.S. Congress, Joint Select Committee on the Condition of Affairs in the Late Insurrectionary States, *Affairs in the Late Insurrectionary States*, vol. 1 (Washington, D.C.: Government Printing Office, 1872; repr., New York: Arno Press, 1969), 180, 369–378. Although Mississippi had abolished slavery in its 1865 constitution prior to the Thirteenth Amendment, Section 2 of the amendment was deeply resented by many in the South because it empowered the U.S. Congress to enforce it. The editorial in the *Vicksburg Daily Herald*, December 12, 1865, considers that provision to violate states' rights.

33. William W. Freehling, *The South vs. the South: How Anti-Confederate Southerners Shaped the Course of the Civil War* (New York: Oxford University Press, 2001), 165–167.

34. Jonathan Truman Dorris, *Pardon and Amnesty under Lincoln and Johnson: The Restoration of the Confederates to Their Rights and Privileges, 1861–1898* (Chapel Hill: University of North Carolina Press, 1953), 221–243; Stanley L. Engerman, "Slavery and Its Consequences for the South in the Nineteenth Century," in *The Cambridge Economic History of the United States*, vol. 2, *The Long Nineteenth Century*, ed. Stanley L. Engerman and Robert E. Gallman, 357 (New York: Cambridge University Press, 2000).

35. See the *Vicksburg Daily Herald* from 1865 through 1867 for the consistently large numbers of notices of foreclosures and forced sales of plantations and advertisements offering plantations for lease.

36. Armyworms are small caterpillars, the larvae of a type of moth, and they have prodigious appetites for cotton plants.

37. Wayne, *Reshaping of Plantation Society*, 75–109.

38. Wayne, *Reshaping of Plantation Society*, 97.

39. C. Vann Woodward, *The Origins of the New South, 1877–1913* (Baton Rouge: Louisiana State University Press, 1951), is the classic analysis of the New South idea.

40. Freehling, *The South vs. the South*, 85–173.

41. Around Vicksburg, the Union army commanders employed blacks on nearby plantations, and Currie, *Enclave*, 83–144, describes how the former plantations of Jefferson and Joseph Davis were the sites of the most successful experiments with entirely freedmen-run enterprises.

42. This point is made by Roark, *Masters without Slaves*, 142. See also Gerald David Jaynes, *Branches without Roots: Genesis of the Black Working Class, 1862–1882* (New York: Oxford University Press, 1986); Engerman, "Slavery and Its Consequences," 357–360.

43. The *Vicksburg Daily Herald*, October 26, 1865, December 5, 1865, February 3, 1866, and February 26, 1867, contains stories about "bad blacks," and the editorial about New Orleans appeared on February 11, 1867. Examples of stories about "good blacks" appeared in the *Vicksburg Daily Herald*, April 14, 20, 1867, and February 11, 1868.

44. For a pre–Civil War example, Daniel Robinson Hundley, *Social Relations in Our Southern States* (New York: Henry B. Price, 1860), 254–258, describes poor whites as "untutored, uncultivated, and servile creatures." He refers to them as "Poor White Trash," a term whose source he attributes to black slaves. The white leadership's recognition of poor whites' dislike for Southern elites was clearly expressed from Mexico by the former governor of Missouri, Thomas C. Reynolds. He characterized President Andrew Johnson as the embodiment of the poor-white spirit of the South, and it was this background, he claimed, that made the president "side against secession, because the wealthier classes supported it." Quoted in Rolle, *Lost Cause*, 150.

45. Keyssar, *Right to Vote*, 112–114; Roark, *Masters without Slaves*, 16–24.

46. Eric Foner, *Reconstruction: America's Unfinished Revolution* (New York: Harper & Row, 1988), 11–18; David Williams, *Bitterly Divided: The South's Inner Civil War* (New York: New Press, 2008). For different aspects of white Southerners' alienation from the Confederacy, see Victoria E. Bynum, "Telling and Retelling the Legend of the 'Free State of Jones,'" in *Guerrillas, Unionists, and Violence on the Confederate Home Front*, ed. Daniel E. Sutherland, 17–29 (Fayetteville: University of Arkansas Press, 1999); Carl N. Degler, *The Other South: Southern Dissenters in the Nineteenth Century* (New York: Harper & Row, 1974), 209–212; Escott, *After Secession*, 94–134; Freehling, *The South vs. the South*; Armstead L. Robinson, *Bitter Fruits of Bondage: The Demise of Slavery and the Collapse of the Confederacy, 1861–1865* (Charlottesville: University of Virginia Press, 2005); David Williams et al., *Plain Folk in a Rich Man's War: Class and Dissent in Confederate Georgia* (Gainesville: University Press of Florida, 2002); Jon L. Wakelyn, *Confederates against the Confederacy: Essays on Leadership and Loyalty* (Westport, Conn.: Praeger, 2002); and Bercaw, *Gendered Freedoms*, 19–93.

47. Elaine Frantz Parsons, "Midnight Rangers: Costume and Performance in the Reconstruction-Era Ku Klux Klan," *Journal of American History* 92 (2005): 811–836.

48. U.S. Congress, *Affairs in the Late Insurrectionary States*, 73–80; Allen W. Trelease, *White Terror: The Ku Klux Klan Conspiracy and Southern Reconstruction* (New York: Harper & Row, 1971), 293–296.

49. Rolle, *Lost Cause*, is the authoritative source for the Confederates' experience in Mexico, and William C. Nunn, *Escape from Reconstruction* (1956; repr., Westport,

Conn.: Greenwood Press, 1974), includes extensive and valuable excerpts from letters and documents.

50. John Ford captured a filmic portrayal of this kind of Southerner in the character of Ethan Edwards in *The Searchers* (1956).

51. The chronicler of General Jo Shelby's brigade's trip to Mexico, with uncharacteristic irony, described those trying to attach themselves to the brigade as "former Generals, Governors, Congressmen, Cabinet officers, men who imagined that the whole power of the United States Government was bent upon their capture," in John N. Edwards, *Shelby's Expedition to Mexico. An Unwritten Leaf of the War*, facsimile reproduction of 1872 edition (Austin, Tex.: Steck, 1964), 14. See Dorris, *Pardon and Amnesty under Lincoln and Johnson*, for the changing terms of pardons and amnesties. William Marshall Anderson, *An American in Maximilian's Mexico, 1865–1866: The Diaries of William Marshall Anderson*, ed. Ramón Eduardo Ruiz (San Marino, Calif.: Huntington Library, 1950); Prince Felix Salm-Salm, *My Diary in Mexico in 1867: Including the Last Days of the Emperor Maximilian; with Leaves from the Diary of Princess Salm-Salm, etc.* (London: R. Bently, 1868); and Alexander Watkins Terrell, *From Texas to Mexico and the Court of Maximilian in 1865* (Dallas: Book Club of Texas, 1933), are informative firsthand accounts of Mexico in Maximilian's time. The first is by a former Texas judge and Confederate general who briefly served as an officer in Maximilian's French army; the second is by a Kentuckian who was employed as a surveyor for Maximilian; and the last is by an Austrian prince who accompanied Maximilian to Mexico.

52. John Mason Hart, *Empire and Revolution: The Americans in Mexico since the Civil War* (Berkeley: University of California Press, 2002), 9–17.

53. Maury had a distinguished career in the U.S. Navy, earned the reputation of a world-class scientist, and was decorated by Maximilian (then head of the Austro-Hungarian navy) for his contributions to naval warfare. Nevertheless, he could not get along with his Confederate colleagues and thus worked as a purchasing agent for the South in London during the Civil War. Rolle, *Lost Cause*, 131–143; Frances Leigh Williams, *Matthew Fontaine Maury: Scientist of the Sea* (New Brunswick, N.J.: Rutgers University Press, 1963). See Jacquelin Ambler Caskie, *Life and Letters of Matthew Fontaine Maury* (Richmond, Va.: Richmond Press, 1928), 55–56, 152–161, for letters concerning Maury's connections with Maximilian and about his work in Mexico.

54. Lawrence F. Hill, "The Confederate Exodus to Latin America, II," *Southwestern Historical Quarterly* 39 (January 1936): 315–319; Nunn, *Escape from Reconstruction*, 80–81.

55. A bloody raid by Indians angry at having lost their land destroyed General Jo Shelby's colony north of Vera Cruz in 1866, reported in Rolle, *Lost Cause*, 110–113.

56. Quoted in Rolle, *Lost Cause*, 186.

57. Nunn, *Escape from Reconstruction*, 82–95, includes extensive excerpts of a diary of a Confederate settler captured, along with twenty-five others, by Juárez's troops and subjected to a forced march to Vera Cruz.

58. Frank A. Knapp Jr., "A New Source on the Confederate Exodus to Mexico: The Two Republics," *Journal of Southern History* 19 (1953): 364–373.

59. The unnamed letter writer was probably Thomas C. Hindman, former Confederate general, an active presence in the early battles in which Swett's Battery participated, and a self-imposed exile in Mexico with former Confederates. For Swett's acquaintance with Hindman, see Swett, "Brief Narrative of Warren Lt. Artillery," 5–8. Diane Neal and

Thomas W. Kremm, *Lion of the South: General Thomas C. Hindman* (Macon, Ga.: Mercer University Press, 1993), 197–218, describes Hindman's experiences in Mexico.

60. Although the *Vicksburg Daily Herald* published several articles on Mexican politics and the colonies of former Confederates there, it was not a reliable source. See the *Vicksburg Daily Herald*, October 28, 29, 1865, November 28, 1865, February 2, 1865, and April 1, 1867. The last article was optimistic about Emperor Maximilian's chances of surviving Juárez's guerrilla assaults, characterizing Maximilian as being "not threatened." In two and a half months, Juárez had prevailed and Maximilian was dead.

61. See, for example, Lawrence F. Hill, *The Confederate Exodus to Latin America* (Austin: Texas State Historical Association, 1936); Blanche Henry Clark Weaver, "Confederate Emigration to Brazil," *Journal of Southern History* 27 (1961): 33–53; Charles Willis Simmons, "Racist Americans in a Multi-Racial Society: Confederate Exiles in Brazil," *Journal of Negro History* 67 (1982): 34–39; William Clark Griggs, *The Elusive Eden: Frank McMullan's Confederate Colony in Brazil* (Austin: University of Texas Press, 1987); Gerald Horne, *The Deepest South: The United States, Brazil, and the African Slave Trade* (New York: New York University Press, 2007); Cyrus B. Dawsey and James M. Dawsey [Brazilian-born descendants of Confederate expatriates], eds., *The Confederados: Old South Immigrants in Brazil* (Tuscaloosa: University of Alabama Press, 1995); and Eugene C. Harter, *The Lost Colony of the Confederacy* (Jackson: University Press of Mississippi, 1985).

62. Cuba was also a slave society at this time, but land was too expensive for all but a fortunate few Southerners, such as "former Confederate secretary of state Judah P. Benjamin, former [U.S.] vice president and U.S. Senator John C. Breckinridge, and Confederate generals Robert Toombs and Jubal Early, as well as wealthy planters such as the McHattons of Louisiana. Matthew Pratt Guterl, "Desengaño: A Confederate Exile in Cuba," in *Race, Nation, and Empire in American History*, ed. James T. Campbell, Matthew Pratt Guterl, and Robert G. Lee, 235 (Chapel Hill: University of North Carolina Press, 2007), lists these eminent former Confederates in Cuba. Cuba was convulsed in a bloody, and eventually futile, ten-year war of independence beginning in 1868. Although Cuban slavery was abolished in 1886, Cubans did not win independence from Spain until 1898.

63. Ballard Dunn, *Brazil: A Home for Southerners* (New York: George B. Richardson, 1866). Written by one of the U.S. entrepreneurs, this is a 272-page description of paradise in Brazil. Along these same lines, see also J. McF. Gaston, *Hunting a Home in Brazil: The Agricultural Resources and other Characteristics of the Country. Also, the Manners and Customs of the Inhabitants* (Philadelphia: King & Baird, Printers, 1867).

64. Simmons, "Racist Americans;" Harter, *Lost Colony of the Confederacy*, 114–118.

65. Alfred Jackson Hanna and Kathryn Abbey Hanna, *Confederate Exiles in Venezuela* (Tuscaloosa, Ala.: Confederate Publishing, 1960), is a clear-eyed study of the Venezuelan project and its sponsors.

66. Hanna and Hanna, *Confederate Exiles in Venezuela*, 23–24.

67. Loreta Janeta Velazquez, *The Woman in Battle: A Narrative of the Exploits, Adventures, and Travels of Loreta Janeta Velazquez* (Richmond, Va.: Dustin, Gilman, 1876); reprinted as *The Woman in Battle: The Civil War Narrative of Loreta Janeta Velazquez, Cuban Woman and Confederate Soldier*, with an introduction by Jesse Alemán (Madison: University of Wisconsin Press, 2003), 536–552. Alemán's introduction and Elizabeth D. Leonard, *All the Daring of the Soldier: Women in the Civil War Armies* (New York: W. W. Norton, 1999), 52–63, discuss the issues of veracity that have surrounded the book since it was published.

68. John Alder Burdon, *Archives of British Honduras*, vol. 3, *From 1841 to 1884* (London: Sifton Praed, 1935), 238.

69. C. H. Grant, *The Making of Modern Belize: Politics, Society and British Colonialism in Central America* (Cambridge: Cambridge University Press, 1976), 30–33, concisely describes the diplomatic disputes that continually swirled around Britain's hold on British Honduras. Capt. G[eorge] Henderson, *An Account of the British Settlement of Honduras* (London: C. and B. Baldwin, 1809), 2–8, reviews, with indignation, the eighteenth-century conflicts with Spain over the settlement, and Burdon, *Archives of British Honduras*, vol. 3, records the continuous Yucatecan raids, their damage, and the government's response. Wayne Clegern expresses the rather dismal quality of this period in the subtitle of his book, *British Honduras: Colonial Dead End, 1859–1900* (Baton Rouge: Louisiana State University Press, 1967). On the other hand, the volume of serious scholarship about British Honduras is impressive.

70. U.S. Consul A. C. Prindle, Dispatch of November 6, 1867, in *Dispatches from United States Consuls in Belize, 1847–1906* (Washington, D.C.: U.S. National Archives and Records Administration), discusses the reasons for the decline in British Honduran exports.

71. For descriptions of these immigrations, see Narda Dobson, *A History of Belize* (London: Longman Caribbean, 1973), 255–256; and Virginia Kerns, "Structural Continuity in the Division of Men's and Women's Work among the Black Carib (Garífuna)," in *Blackness in Latin America and the Caribbean: Social Dynamics and Cultural Transformations*, vol. 1, *Central America and Northern and Western Southern America*, ed. Norman E. Whitten and Arlene Torres, 133–148 (Bloomington: Indiana University Press, 1998). The original Caribs were one of the dominant tribes in and around the Caribbean before the Spanish conquest. Most died due to disease and mistreatment, and in the nineteenth and twentieth centuries it became common for North Americans and Europeans to call a culturally distinct group of mixed African and indigenous peoples on the Caribbean coasts of Nicaragua, Honduras, Guatemala, and British Honduras "Black Caribs." They call themselves "Garífuna." Rebecca B. Bateman, "Africans and Indians: A Comparative Study of the Black Carib and Black Seminole [Honduras, Belize, Florida]," in Whitten and Torres, *Blackness in Latin America and the Caribbean*, vol. 1, 200–222.

72. Burdon, *Archives of British Honduras*, vol. 3, 201.

73. After 200 years of indecision, the British government elevated the status of British Honduras from "settlement" to "colony" in 1862; see Herbert F. Curry Jr., "British Honduras: From Public Meeting to Crown Colony," *The Americas* 13 (1956): 31–42. The newly designated colony therefore had a lieutenant governor, reporting to the governor of Jamaica, as the chief executive. The lieutenant governor also worked with an elected legislative assembly. See U.S. Department of State, "Correspondence between Great Britain and the United States, in Relation to Central American Affairs," in *Documents Relative to Central American Affairs and the Enlistment Question* (Washington, D.C.: C. Wendell, Printer, 1856), 5–241, for a record of U.S. officials' unease about the prospect of British Honduras becoming a formal colony of Great Britain's.

74. Burdon, *Archives of British Honduras*, vol. 3, 146.

75. For the efforts to recruit freed slaves from the United States to emigrate to British Honduras, see Clegern, *British Honduras*, 33–37; Janet L. Coryell, "'The Lincoln Colony': Aaron Columbus Burr's Proposed Colonization of British Honduras," *Civil War History* 43 (1997): 5–15; and Burdon, *Archives of British Honduras*, vol. 3, 254.

76. Most of the mid-nineteenth-century colonization schemes focused on Mexico, Central America, or the Caribbean as potential sites. Michael Vorenberg, "Abraham Lincoln and the Politics of Black Colonization," *Journal of the Abraham Lincoln Association* 14 (1993): 23–45, is good on the general U.S. politics surrounding the colonization initiatives. Warren Beck, "Lincoln and Negro Colonization in Central America," *Abraham Lincoln Quarterly* 6 (September 1950): 162–183, describes the efforts to establish a colony in Panama; and James D. Lockett, "Abraham Lincoln and Colonization: An Episode that Ends in Tragedy at L'Ile àVache, Haiti, 1863–1864," *Journal of Black Studies* 21 (1991): 428–444, recounts the disastrous venture of U.S. freedmen on the Haitian island of L'Ille à Vach. Thomas Schoonover, "Misconstrued Mission: Expansionism and Black Colonization in Mexico and Central America during the Civil War," *Pacific Historical Review* 49 (1980): 607–620, focuses on the resistance by Mexican and Central American leaders to the proposals. On the Lincoln administration's reluctant abandonment of colonization, see Sharon Hartman Strom, "Labor, Race and Colonization: Imagining a Post-Slavery World in the Americas," in *The Problem of Evil: Slavery, Race and the Ambiguities of Reform*, ed. Steven Mintz and John Stauffer, 260–275 (Amherst: University of Massachusetts Press, 2007).

77. U.S. Consul Charles A. Leas, Dispatch of September 12, 1864, in *Dispatches from United States Consuls in Belize, 1847–1906*, reviews and renews his resistance to sending free blacks to Belize. This report is only one of several that expressed irritation at the lieutenant governor's continuing interest in such a project despite the British government's explicit prohibition, noted in Burdon, *Archives of British Honduras*, vol. 3, 254. Charles A. Leas, Dispatch of August 12, 1864, in *Dispatches from United States Consuls in Belize, 1847–1906*, describes British Honduras's draconian labor laws.

78. Burdon, *Archives of British Honduras*, vol. 3, 264, 310, 313, 314, 317. Guterl, "Desengaño," 238–243, describes a similarly disastrous experience by Chinese contract workers in Cuba.

79. Clegern, *British Honduras*, 33–41; Donald C. Simmons Jr., *Confederate Settlements in British Honduras* (Jefferson, N.C.: McFarland, 2001), 22–32.

80. U.S. Consul A. C. Prindle, Dispatch of August 9, 1867, in *Dispatches from United States Consuls in Belize, 1847–1906*, describes the reasons for Austin's recall and his unpopularity within British Honduras.

81. U.S. Consul Charles A. Leas, Dispatches of March 10, 1864, and April 1, 1864, in *Dispatches from United States Consuls in Belize, 1847–1906*, reports the arrival of sizable groups of former Confederates who in 1864 already believed that the war was lost. U.S. Consul A. C. Prindle, Dispatches of August 9, 1867, and November 6, 1867, are the sources for the estimates of immigration rates.

82. For a description of a dangerous and grueling trip from Texas to Brazil, see Sarah Bellona, "The American Colonies Emigrating to Brazil—1865," in Dawsey and Dawsey, *Confederados*, 27–33.

83. For news about the *Trade Wind*, see U.S. Consul A. C. Prindle, Dispatches of August 9, 1867, and November 8, 1869, in *Dispatches from United States Consuls in Belize, 1847–1906*. On seasickness as a common trope among nineteenth-century travelers, see Brian Roberts, *American Alchemy: The California Gold Rush and Middle-Class Culture* (Chapel Hill: University of North Carolina Press, 2000), 96–99.

84. U.S. War Department, *The War of the Rebellion: A Compilation of the Official Records of the Union and Confederate Armies* (Washington, D.C.: Government Printing Office, 1880–1901).

85. Francis Drake, *Dictionary of American Biography* (Boston: J. R. Osgood, 1872); James Grant Wilson and John Fiske, eds., *Appleton's Cyclopaedia of American Biography*, 8 vols. (New York: D. Appleton, 1887); *National Cyclopedia of American Biography* (1898–). INDEX. (Clifton, N.J.: James T. White, 1984).

86. U.S. Consul A. C. Prindle, Dispatch of January 1, 1868, in *Dispatches from United States Consuls in Belize, 1847–1906.*

87. Mary Louise Pratt, *Imperial Eyes: Travel Writing and Transculturation* (New York: Routledge, 1992), 148.

88. Charles Swett's travelogue was unusual for its inattention to the erotic charms of Central American women but similar in its assumption that white women did not belong in the region. Amy Greenberg, *Manifest Manhood and the Antebellum Empire* (New York: Cambridge University Press, 2005), 112–134, 211–221.

89. Quoted in Simmons, *Confederate Settlements in British Honduras*, 57. General Benjamin Butler was the Union army commander during the capture of New Orleans, and he became the military governor of the southern Mississippi Valley. He was not popular among former Confederates. U.S. consular reports are also clear about the resentment of the local population toward the attitudes and behavior of Southern immigrants. See U.S. Counsel A. C. Prindle, Dispatches of January 1, 1870, and April 12, 1870, in *Dispatches from United States Consuls in Belize, 1847–1906.*

90. Burdon, *Archives of British Honduras*, vol. 3, 298–301. "Coloured" people are of mixed race, a distinction generally not made in the United States, where most whites regarded people of any combination of ancestry that included African as black.

91. Burdon, *Archives of British Honduras*, vol. 3, 330.

92. Simmons, *Confederate Settlements in British Honduras*, 56–58.

93. Burdon, *Archives of British Honduras*, vol. 3, 302; Simmons, *Confederate Settlements in British Honduras*, 70–86.

94. Burdon, *Archives of British Honduras*, vol. 3, 306.

95. John Lloyd Stephens, *Incidents of Travel in Central America, Chiapas, and Yucatán* (London: John Murray, 1841); Robert Glasgow Dunlop, *Travels in Central America, being a Journal of nearly three years' Residence in the Country* (London: Longman, Brown, Green, and Longmans, 1847); William V. Wells, *Explorations and Adventures in Honduras* (New York: Harper & Bros., 1857); Julius Froebel, *Seven Years Travel in Central America, Northern Mexico, and the Far West of the United States* (London: Richard Bentley, 1859); and Ephraim George Squier, *The States of Central America* (New York: Harper & Bros., 1858), are examples of books that were popular in the United States and fairly current at that time. Franklin D. Parker, *Travels in Central America, 1821–1840* (Gainesville: University of Florida Press, 1970), 321–324, is a good bibliography of nineteenth-century Central American travel literature, with a striking lack of any reference to British Honduras.

In his "Conclusion," Swett perceptively states, "Much has been written concerning Honduras, that presented the appearance of speculation, and not unfrequently *by Speculators.*" There are, however, no citations, and since he had not planned to go to Honduras, his acquaintance with some writings on Spanish Central America must have occurred after his return to Mississippi.

96. Joseph P. Lockey, "Diplomatic Futility," *Hispanic American Historical Review* 10 (1930): 265–294, exaggerates the inept and disastrous efforts by the U.S. government to establish a diplomatic presence in Central America during the 1830s and 1840s. For example, the reports by the second U.S. charge d'affaires to Central America, Charles G.

De Witt, between April 30, 1833, and October 6, 1838, are surprisingly lucid and informative about the continuing chaos of the region. See William R. Manning, ed., *Diplomatic Correspondence of the United States, Inter-American Affairs, 1831–1860*, vol. 3, *Central America, 1831–1850* (Washington, D.C.: Carnegie Endowment for International Peace, 1933), 70–156.

97. Charles L. Stansifer, "E. George Squier and the Honduras Interoceanic Railroad Project," *Hispanic American Historical Review* 46 (1966): 1–27; Sharon Hartman Strom, "E. G. Squier y el Ferrocarril Oceánico Hondureño: Centro América en la Imaginación Norteamericana," *Yaxkin* 14 (October 1996): 127–137.

98. Robert E. May, *Manifest Destiny's Underworld: Filibustering in Antebellum America* (Chapel Hill: University of North Carolina Press, 2002), 254–279, emphasizes the increasingly close identification between filibustering and Southern sectionalism during the 1850s.

99. Héctor Pérez Brignoli, "Economía y sociedad en Honduras durante el siglo XIX: Las estructuras demográficas," *Estudios Sociales Centroamericanas* 6 (1973): 53–54, 58–59.

100. For background on Spanish-speaking Central America, see Ciro Cardoso and Héctor Pérez Brignoli, *Centroamérica y la economía occidental (1520–1930)* (San José, Costa Rica: Editorial Universidad, 1977); Julio César Pinto Soria, *Centroamérica de la colonia al estado nacional (1800–1840)* (Guatemala: Editorial Universitaria de Guatemala, 1986); Mario Rodriguez, *A Palmerstonian Diplomat in Central America: Frederick Chatfield, Esq.* (Tucson: University of Arizona Press, 1964); Frederick Stirton Weaver, *Inside the Volcano: History and Political Economy of Central America* (Boulder, Colo.: Westview Press, 1994); Frederick Stirton Weaver, "Reform and (Counter-)Revolution in Post-Independence Guatemala: Liberalism, Conservatism, and Postmodern Controversies," *Latin American Perspectives* 26 (1999): 129–158; Ralph Lee Woodward, *Rafael Carrera and the Emergence of the Republic of Guatemala, 1821–1871* (Athens: University of Georgia Press, 1993); and Ralph Lee Woodward, *Central America: A Nation Divided*, 3rd ed. (New York: Oxford University Press, 1999). Marvin Barahona, *Evolución histórica de la identidad nacional* (Tegucigalpa: Editorial Guaymuras, 1991); Dario A. Euraque, *Estado, poder, nacionalidad y raza en la historia de Honduras: Ensayos* (Choluteca, Honduras: Ediciones Subiriama, 1996); and Pablo Yankelavic, *Honduras: Una breve historia* (México, D.F.: Instituto de Investigaciones Dr. José Maria Luis Mora, Universidad de Guadalajara, 1988), focus on Honduran history, and Rodolfo Pastor Fasquelle, *Biografía de San Pedro Sula, 1536–1954* (San Pedro Sula, Honduras: Centro Editorial, 1990), is a very helpful history of San Pedro Sula.

101. Leopoldo Zea, *The Latin American Mind* (Norman: University of Oklahoma Press, 1963), 37–87; for a Liberal example, see Domingo Faustino Sarmiento, *Life in the Argentine Republic in the Days of the Tyrants, or Civilization and Barbarism* [1843] (New York: Collier Books, 1961).

102. Carol A. Smith, "Origins of the National Question in Guatemala, a Hypothesis," in *Guatemalan Indians and the State, 1540–1988* (Austin: University of Texas Press, 1990), 72–95.

103. The current capital city—Tegucigalpa—became the capital in 1873.

104. Stansifer, "E. George Squier"; Strom, "E. G. Squier."

105. No doubt Swett meant Puerto Caballos, which was subsequently renamed Puerto Cortés, named after Hernán Cortés, who led the Spanish conquest of the Aztec capital, Tenochtitlan (now Mexico City), in 1521. He visited Honduras briefly to mediate disputes among competing claims by groups of Spaniards. Puerto Caballos/Cortés is seven miles east of Omoa and would become the northern terminus of the railroad to San Pedro Sula.

106. There are conflicting stories about why the McDermott family's foray to Honduras was a failure, but they agree that it was a failure. See www.seaark.net~sabra/der.html and www.seaark.net/~sabra/Lzbiog.html for the contrasting stories.

107. José Reynaud immigrated to San Pedro Sula, Honduras, from France in the 1860s. He was a literate, trilingual merchant active in local politics. Contrary to Swett's impression, however, Pastor Fasquelle, *Biografía de San Pedro Sula*, 208, says that Reynaud was not a governor but rather the municipal secretary and former alcalde of San Pedro Sula. Reynaud translated the documents included in Appendix A.

108. Pastor Fasquelle, *Biografía de San Pedro Sula*, 153–179, describes the arrival of the Confederates. The U.S. consul in Omoa, Charles R. Follin, Dispatch of September 30, 1867, in *Dispatches from United States Consuls in Omoa, Truxillo, and Ruatan, Honduras, 1818 to 1880*, Roll 3: January 12, 1858, to December 31, 1869 (Washington, D.C.: U.S. National Archives and Records Administration), unflatteringly portrayed them as being "principally the lower class of southern people." Another set of foreigners arrived in San Pedro Sula around the same time as the former Confederates. They were French and German "soldiers of fortune" who had fought for Maximilian in Mexico and were unemployed after his defeat. Pastor Fasquelle, *Biografía de San Pedro Sula*, 12–13, 208–209, believes that they also fought for conservative politicians in Honduras but soon became leading citizens of the village.

109. Pastor Fasquelle, *Biografía de San Pedro Sula*, 12–13.

110. The following information on Major Green Malcolm is from Margaret Malcolm Haas, great-granddaughter of Green Malcolm. She was kind enough to send us three informative e-mails about Green Malcolm on August 10, 11, and 19, 2005. This information was importantly augmented by a long e-mail on August 12, 2005, from Elwood Coleman, formerly of San Pedro Sula.

111. For information on the 1st Tennessee Cavalry and Malcolm's membership, see www.tngennet.org/civilwar/csacav/csamcnairy.html.

112. The dispatch is from U.S. Consul Frank E. Frye, Dispatch of September 30, 1875, in *Dispatches from United States Consuls in Omoa, Truxillo, and Ruatan, 1818 to 1890*, Roll 4: March 31, 1870, to September 16, 1880. The "insect to them unknown" conflicts with Swett's confident identification of insect egg clusters on Malcolm's cotton plants as being armyworms.

113. The following material on the Coleman family is from Elwood Coleman's Web site, coleman-young.blogspot.com. He was born in San Pedro Sula and is a great-great-grandson of William Allen Coleman. We are also grateful for helpful personal communications from him on August 12, 2005, and April 2, 2008.

114. Pastor Fasquelle, *Biografía de San Pedro Sula*, 181–182.

115. Pastor Fasquelle, *Biografía de San Pedro Sula*, 234.

116. Pastor Fasquelle, *Biografía de San Pedro Sula*, 209.

117. Pastor Fasquelle, *Biografía de San Pedro Sula*, 207, 194, 243.

118. The information about James M. Putnam comes from the Web site of one of his descendants, www.billputnam.com. Simmons, *Confederate Settlements in British Honduras*, 61, reports on the other returnees.

PART III

1. Lawrence F. Hill, "The Confederate Exodus to Latin America, I," *Southwestern Historical Quarterly* 39 (October 1935): 173–175; Riccardo Orizio, *Lost White Tribes: Journeys among the Forgotten* (London: Secker and Warburg, 2000), 96–123.

2. Andrew F. Rolle, *The Lost Cause: The Confederate Exodus to Mexico* (Norman: University of Oklahoma Press, 1965), 116.

3. Donald C. Simmons Jr., *Confederate Settlements in British Honduras* (Jefferson, N.C.: McFarland, 2001), 82.

4. David McCreery, *Rural Guatemala, 1760–1940* (Stanford, Calif.: Stanford University Press, 1994), is an excellent study of the development of the debt peonage system in Guatemala. U.S. Consul Charles A. Leas, Dispatch of March 10, 1864, in *Dispatches from United States Consuls in Belize, 1847–1906* (Washington, D.C.: U.S. National Archives and Records Administration), describes the harsh labor laws prevailing in British Honduras at this time.

5. John Alder Burdon, *Archives of British Honduras*, vol. 3, *From 1841 to 1884* (London: Sifton Praed, 1935).

6. Quoted in Lawrence F. Hill, "The Confederate Exodus to Latin America, II," *Southwestern Historical Quarterly* 39 (January 1936): 177, 180.

7. Rolle, *Lost Cause*, 172.

8. B. R. Duval, *A Narrative of Life and Travels in Mexico and British Honduras* (Richmond, Va.: Clemmit & Jones, 1878), 43–75, graphically describes the difficulties that he and his family faced just getting by in the British Honduran countryside.

9. U.S. Consul A. C. Prindle, Dispatches of July 1, 1867, January 10, 1868, June 1, 1869, and January 29, 1870, in *Dispatches from United States Consuls in Belize, 1847–1906*, comments on the problems with penniless former Confederates trying to return to the United States from British Honduras; and Simmons, *Confederate Settlements in British Honduras*, 56–61, describes the issues raised by these people. The quotation about the return of the former Confederates in Honduras is in U.S. Consul Frank E. Frye, Dispatch of September 30, 1875, in *Dispatches from United States Consuls in Omoa, Truxillo, and Ruatan, 1818 to 1890*, Roll 4: March 31, 1870, to September 16, 1880 (Washington, D.C.: U.S. National Archives and Records Administration).

10. Brainerd Dyer, "The Persistence of the Idea of Negro Colonization," *Pacific Historical Review* 12 (1943): 55; Carl N. Degler, *The Other South: Southern Dissenters in the Nineteenth Century* (New York: Harper & Row, 1974), 21–25; Darlene Clark Hine et al., *African Americans: A Concise History* [combined volume] (Upper Saddle River, N.J.: Prentice Hall, 2004), 124–126.

11. Degler, *The Other South*, 21–25, passim.

12. James L. Roark, *Masters without Slaves: Southern Planters in the Civil War and Reconstruction* (New York: W. W. Norton, 1977), 168–169. While one delegate to the 1865 Mississippi state constitutional convention proposed "colonizing" newly freed African Americans, the idea was not discussed. *Journal of the Proceedings and Debates in*

the Constitutional Convention of the State of Mississippi, August 1865 (Jackson, Miss.: E. M. Yerger, State Printer, 1865), 247.

13. Sharon Hartman Strom, "Labor, Race and Colonization: Imagining a Post-Slavery World in the Americas," in *The Problem of Evil: Slavery, Race and the Ambiguities of Reform*, ed. Steven Mintz and John Stauffer, 270 (Amherst: University of Massachusetts Press, 2007).

14. C. Vann Woodward, *Reunion and Reaction: The Compromise of 1877 and the End of Reconstruction* (Boston: Little, Brown, 1966), is a brilliant analysis of the Compromise of 1877 that led to the end of Reconstruction.

15. Nell Irvin Painter, *Exodusters: Black Migration to Kansas after Reconstruction* (Lawrence: University Press of Kansas, 1986), 82–92, 137–141.

16. Painter, *Exodusters*, 147–201.

17. Painter, *Exodusters*, 237.

18. Michael Wayne, *The Reshaping of Plantation Society: The Natchez District, 1860–1880* (Baton Rouge: Louisiana State University Press, 1983), 60–61; Ronald Takaki, *Strangers from a Different Shore: A History of Asian Americans* (New York: Penguin Books, 1989), 94–95.

19. Richard Aubrey McLemore, *A History of Mississippi* (Hattiesburg: University and College Press of Mississippi, 1973), 605.

20. The information on the patents is from coleman-young.blogspot.com; for the patent litigation, see William Burrnam Woods, *Cases Argued and Determined in the Circuit Courts of the United States for the Fifth Judicial District* (Chicago: Callaghan, 1875), 138–143. The U.S. Office of the Commissioners of Claims interviewed Vicksburg people about Daniel's worthiness, and the answers are inconsistent and evasive. See www.footnote.com/image/1082; www.footnote.com/image/11098; www.footnote.com/image/1100; www.footnote.com/image/1102; www.footnote.com/image/1104; and www.footnote.com/image/1108, all accessed October 16, 2007. The *Vicksburg Times and Republican*, December 24, 1871, is almost gleeful in reporting locals' successes with the Southern Claims Commission.

21. James F. Brieger, *Hometown Mississippi* (Jackson, Miss.: Town Square Books, 1997), 182.

22. Eric Foner, *Reconstruction: America's Unfinished Revolution* (New York: Harper & Row, 1988), 512–601.

23. David W. Blight, *Race and Reunion: The Civil War in American Memory* (Cambridge, Mass.: Harvard University Press, 2001), 140–170; Christopher Waldrep, *Vicksburg's Long Shadow: The Civil War Legacy of Race and Remembrance* (Lanham, Md.: Rowman & Littlefield, 2005), 102–139.

24. Nina Silber, *The Romance of Reunion: Northerners and the South, 1865–1900* (Chapel Hill: University of North Carolina Press, 1993); Gary W. Gallagher and Alan T. Nolan, *The Myth of the Lost Cause and Civil War History* (Bloomington: Indiana University Press, 2000); Waldrep, *Vicksburg's Long Shadow*; Gaines M. Foster, *Ghosts of the Confederacy: Defeat, the Lost Cause, and the Emergence of the New South, 1865 to 1913* (New York: Oxford University Press, 1987), 115–126, 180–198; and especially Blight, *Race and Reunion*, are good treatments of the ways in which representations of the U.S. Civil War have obscured the role of slavery and black emancipation.

25. Waldrep, *Vicksburg's Long Shadow*, 168.

26. Waldrep, *Vicksburg's Long Shadow*, 180.

Selected References

Primary and secondary sources for our central themes of migration, colonization, race, and Confederates in Mexico, Central America, and South America are listed below. Well-known sources on the history of Mississippi, the Civil War, and Reconstruction are fully cited in our endnotes and are omitted here.

Anderson, William Marshall. *An American in Maximilian's Mexico, 1865–1866: The Diaries of William Marshall Anderson.* Edited by Ramón Eduardo Ruiz. San Marino, Calif.: Huntington Library, 1950.

Barahona, Marvin. *Evolución histórica de la identidad nacional.* Tegucigalpa: Editorial Guaymuras, 1991.

Bateman, Rebecca B. "Africans and Indians: A Comparative Study of the Black Carib and Black Seminole [Honduras, Belize, Florida]." In *Blackness in Latin America and the Caribbean: Social Dynamics and Cultural Transformations.* Vol. 1, *Central America and Northern and Western Southern America,* edited by Norman E. Whitten and Arlene Torres, 200–222. Bloomington: Indiana University Press, 1998.

Beck, Warren. "Lincoln and Negro Colonization in Central America." *Abraham Lincoln Quarterly* 6 (September 1950): 162–183.

Bellona, Sarah. "The American Colonies Emigrating to Brazil—1865." In *The Confederados: Old South Immigrants in Brazil,* edited by Cyrus B. Dawsey and James M. Dawsey, 26–49. Tuscaloosa: University of Alabama Press, 1995.

Burdon, John Alder. *Archives of British Honduras.* Vol. 2, *From 1801 to 1840.* London: Sifton Praed, 1934.

———. *Archives of British Honduras.* Vol. 3, *From 1841 to 1884.* London: Sifton Praed, 1935.

Cardoso, Ciro, and Héctor Pérez Brignoli. *Centroamérica y la economía occidental (1520–1930).* San José, Costa Rica: Editorial Universidad, 1977.

Caskie, Jacquelin Ambler. *Life and Letters of Matthew Fontaine Maury.* Richmond, Va.: Richmond Press, 1928.

Clegern, Wayne M. *British Honduras: Colonial Dead End, 1859–1900.* Baton Rouge: Louisiana State University Press, 1967.

Coryell, Janet L. "'The Lincoln Colony': Aaron Columbus Burr's Proposed Colonization of British Honduras." *Civil War History* 43 (1997): 5–15.

Dawsey, Cyrus B., and James M. Dawsey. *The Confederados: Old South Immigrants in Brazil.* Tuscaloosa: University of Alabama Press, 1995.

Dobson, Narda. *A History of Belize.* London: Longman Caribbean, 1973.

Dunlop, Robert Glasgow. *Travels in Central America, being a Journal of nearly Three years' Residence in the Country.* London: Longman, Brown, Green, and Longmans, 1847.

Dunn, Ballard. *Brazil: A Home for Southerners.* New York: George B. Richardson, 1866.

Duval, B. R. *A Narrative of Life and Travels in Mexico and British Honduras.* Richmond, Va.: Clemmit & Jones, 1878.

Dyer, Brainerd. "The Persistence of the Idea of Negro Colonization." *Pacific Historical Review* 12 (1943): 53–65.

Edwards, John N. *Shelby's Expedition to Mexico: An Unwritten Leaf of the War.* Facsimile reproduction of 1872 edition. Austin, Tex.: Steck, 1964.

Euraque, Dario A. *Estado, poder, nacionalidad y raza en la historia de Honduras: Ensayos.* Choluteca, Honduras: Ediciones Subiriama, 1996.

Follin, Charles R. Dispatch of September 30, 1867. In *Dispatches from United States Consuls in Omoa, Truxillo, and Ruatan, Honduras, 1818 to 1880.* Roll 3: January 12, 1858, to December 31, 1869. Washington, D.C.: U.S. National Archives and Records Administration.

Froebel, Julius. *Seven Years Travel in Central America, Northern Mexico, and the Far West of the United States.* London: Richard Bentley, 1859.

Frye, Frank E. Dispatch of September 30, 1875. In *Dispatches from United States Consuls in Omoa, Truxillo, and Ruatan, 1818 to 1890.* Roll 4: March 31, 1870, to September 16, 1880. Washington, D.C.: U.S. National Archives and Records Administration.

Gaston, J. McF. *Hunting a Home in Brazil: The Agricultural Resources and other Characteristics of the Country. Also, the Manners and Customs of the Inhabitants.* Philadelphia: King & Baird, Printers, 1867.

Grant, C. H. *The Making of Modern Belize: Politics, Society and British Colonialism in Central America.* Cambridge: Cambridge University Press, 1976.

Griggs, William Clark. *The Elusive Eden: Frank McMullan's Confederate Colony in Brazil.* Austin: University of Texas Press, 1987.

Guterl, Matthew Pratt. "Desengaño: A Confederate Exile in Cuba." In *Race, Nation, and Empire in American History,* ed. James T. Campbell, Matthew Pratt Guterl, and Robert G. Lee, 231–241. Chapel Hill: University of North Carolina Press, 2007.

Hanna, Alfred Jackson, and Kathryn Abbey Hanna. *Confederate Exiles in Venezuela.* Tuscaloosa, Ala.: Confederate Publishing, 1960.

Hart, John Mason. *Empire and Revolution: The Americans in Mexico since the Civil War.* Berkeley: University of California Press, 2002.

Harter, Eugene C. *The Lost Colony of the Confederacy.* Jackson: University Press of Mississippi, 1985.

Henderson, Capt. G[eorge]. *An Account of the British Settlement of Honduras.* London: C. and B. Baldwin, 1809.

Hill, Lawrence F. "The Confederate Exodus to Latin America, I." *Southwestern Historical Quarterly* 39 (October 1935): 100–134.

———. "The Confederate Exodus to Latin America, II." *Southwestern Historical Quarterly* 39 (January 1936): 161–199.

———. "The Confederate Exodus to Latin America, III." *Southwestern Historical Quarterly* 39 (April 1936): 309–326.

[The three articles were reprinted as Hill, Lawrence F., *The Confederate Exodus to Latin America*. Austin: Texas State Historical Association, 1936.]

Horne, Gerald. *The Deepest South: The United States, Brazil, and the African Slave Trade*. New York: New York University Press, 2007.

Kerns, Virginia. "Structural Continuity in the Division of Men's and Women's Work among the Black Carib (Garífuna) [Belize]." In *Blackness in Latin America and the Caribbean: Social Dynamics and Cultural Transformations*. Vol. 1, *Central America and Northern and Western Southern America*, ed. Norman E. Whitten and Arlene Torres, 133–148. Bloomington: Indiana University Press, 1998.

Knapp, Frank A., Jr. "A New Source on the Confederate Exodus to Mexico: The Two Republics." *Journal of Southern History* 19 (1953): 364–373.

Leas, Charles A. Dispatch of March 10, 1864. In *Dispatches from United States Consuls in Belize, 1847–1906*. Washington, D.C.: U.S. National Archives and Records Administration.

———. Dispatch of April 1, 1864. In *Dispatches from United States Consuls in Belize, 1847–1906*. Washington, D.C.: U.S. National Archives and Records Administration.

———. Dispatch of August 12, 1864. In *Dispatches from United States Consuls in Belize, 1847–1906*. Washington, D.C.: U.S. National Archives and Records Administration.

———. Dispatch of September 12, 1864. In *Dispatches from United States Consuls in Belize, 1847–1906*. Washington, D.C.: U.S. National Archives and Records Administration.

Lockett, James D. "Abraham Lincoln and Colonization: An Episode that Ends in Tragedy at L'Ile àVache, Haiti, 1863–1864." *Journal of Black Studies* 21 (1991): 428–444.

Lockey, Joseph P. "Diplomatic Futility." *Hispanic American Historical Review* 10 (1930): 265–294.

Mack, Gerstle. *The Land Divided: A History of the Panama Canal and Other Isthmian Canal Projects*. New York: Alfred A. Knopf, 1944.

Manning, William R., ed. *Diplomatic Correspondence of the United States, Inter-American Affairs, 1831–1860*. Vol. 3, *Central America, 1831–1850*. Washington, D.C.: Carnegie Endowment for International Peace, 1933.

May, Robert E. *Manifest Destiny's Underworld: Filibustering in Antebellum America*. Chapel Hill: University of North Carolina Press, 2002.

McCreery, David. *Rural Guatemala, 1760–1940*. Stanford, Calif.: Stanford University Press, 1994.

McGuinness, Aims. *Path of Empire: Panama and the California Gold Rush*. Ithaca, N.Y.: Cornell University Press, 2008.

Neal, Diane, and Thomas W. Kremm. *Lion of the South: General Thomas C. Hindman*. Macon, Ga.: Mercer University Press, 1993.

Nunn, William C. *Escape from Reconstruction*. 1956. Reprint, Westport, Conn.: Greenwood Press, 1974.

Orizio, Riccardo. *Lost White Tribes: Journeys among the Forgotten*. London: Secker and Warburg, 2000.

Painter, Nell Irvin. *Exodusters: Black Migration to Kansas after Reconstruction*. Lawrence: University Press of Kansas, 1986.

Parker, Franklin D. *Travels in Central America, 1821–1840.* Gainesville: University of Florida Press, 1970.

Pastor Fasquelle, Rodolfo. *Biografía de San Pedro Sula, 1536–1954.* San Pedro Sula, Honduras: Centro Editorial, 1990.

Pérez Brignoli, Héctor. "Economía y sociedad en Honduras durante el siglo XIX: Las estructuras demográficas." *Estudios Sociales Centroamericanas* 6 (1973): 51–63.

Pinto Soria, Julio César. *Centroamérica de la colonia al estado nacional (1800–1840).* Guatemala: Editorial Universitaria de Guatemala, 1986.

Pratt, Mary Louise. *Imperial Eyes: Travel Writing and Transculturation.* New York: Routledge, 1992.

Prindle, A. C. Dispatch of August 9, 1867. In *Dispatches from United States Consuls in Belize, 1847–1906.* Washington, D.C.: U.S. National Archives and Records Administration.

———. Dispatch of November 6, 1867. In *Dispatches from United States Consuls in Belize, 1847–1906.* Washington, D.C.: U.S. National Archives and Records Administration.

———. Dispatch of January 1, 1868. In *Dispatches from United States Consuls in Belize, 1847–1906.* Washington, D.C.: U.S. National Archives and Records Administration.

———. Dispatch of June 1, 1869. In *Dispatches from United States Consuls in Belize, 1847–1906.* Washington, D.C.: U.S. National Archives and Records Administration.

———. Dispatch of November 8, 1869. In *Dispatches from United States Consuls in Belize, 1847–1906.* Washington, D.C.: U.S. National Archives and Records Administration.

———. Dispatch of January 1, 1870. In *Dispatches from United States Consuls in Belize, 1847–1906.* Washington, D.C.: U.S. National Archives and Records Administration.

———. Dispatch of April 12, 1870. In *Dispatches from United States Consuls in Belize, 1847–1906.* Washington, D.C.: U.S. National Archives and Records Administration.

Ransom, Roger. *One Kind of Freedom: The Economic Consequences of Emancipation.* New York: Cambridge University Press, 1977.

Rodriguez, Mario. *A Palmerstonian Diplomat in Central America: Frederick Chatfield, Esq.* Tucson: University of Arizona Press, 1964.

Rolle, Andrew F. *The Lost Cause: The Confederate Exodus to Mexico.* Norman: University of Oklahoma Press, 1965.

Salm-Salm, Felix, Prinz zu. *My diary in Mexico in 1867: Including the Last Days of the Emperor Maximilian; with Leaves from the Diary of Princess Salm-Salm, etc.* London: R. Bently, 1868.

Schoonover, Thomas. "Misconstrued Mission: Expansionism and Black Colonization in Mexico and Central America during the Civil War." *Pacific Historical Review* 49 (1980): 607–620.

Simmons, Charles Willis. "Racist Americans in a Multi-Racial Society: Confederate Exiles in Brazil." *Journal of Negro History* 67 (1982): 34–39.

Simmons, Donald C., Jr. *Confederate Settlements in British Honduras.* Jefferson, N.C.: McFarland, 2001.

Squier, Ephraim George. *The States of Central America.* New York: Harper & Bros., 1858.

Stansifer, Charles L. "E. George Squier and the Honduras Interoceanic Railroad Project." *Hispanic American Historical Review* 46 (1966): 1–27.

Stephens, John Lloyd. *Incidents of Travel in Central America, Chiapas, and Yucatán.* London: John Murray, 1841.

Strom, Sharon Hartman. "E. G. Squier y el Ferrocarril Oceánico Hondureño: Centro América en la Imaginación Norteamericana." *Yaxkin* 14 (October 1996): 127–137.

———. "Labor, Race and Colonization: Imagining a Post-Slavery World in the Americas." In *The Problem of Evil: Slavery, Race and the Ambiguities of Reform,* ed. Steven Mintz and John Stauffer, 260–275. Amherst: University of Massachusetts Press, 2007.

Sutherland, Daniel E. *The Confederate Carpetbaggers.* Baton Rouge: Louisiana State University Press, 1988.

———. "Exiles, Emigrants, and Sojourners: The Post-Civil War Confederate Exodus in Perspective." *Civil War History* 31 (1985): 237–256.

———. "Looking for a Home." *Louisiana History* 21 (1980): 341–359.

Terrell, Alexander Watkins. *From Texas to Mexico and the Court of Maximilian in 1865.* Dallas: Book Club of Texas, 1933.

U.S. Department of State. "Correspondence between Great Britain and the United States, in Relation to Central American Affairs." In *Documents Relative to Central American Affairs and the Enlistment Question.* Washington, D.C.: C. Wendell, Printer, 1856.

Velazquez, Loreta Janeta. *The Woman in Battle: A Narrative of the Exploits, Adventures, and Travels of Loreta Janeta Velazquez.* Richmond, Va.: Dustin, Gilman, 1876. Reprinted as *The Woman in Battle: The Civil War Narrative of Loreta Janeta Velazquez, Cuban Woman and Confederate Soldier.* Introduction by Jesse Alemán. Madison: University of Wisconsin Press, 2003.

Vorenberg, Michael. "Abraham Lincoln and the Politics of Black Colonization." *Journal of the Abraham Lincoln Association* 14 (1993): 23–45.

Waddell, D. A. G. *British Honduras: A Historical and Contemporary Survey.* Westport, Conn.: Greenwood Press, 1981.

Weaver, Blanche Henry Clark. "Confederate Emigration to Brazil." *Journal of Southern History* 27 (1961): 33–53.

Weaver, Frederick Stirton. *Inside the Volcano: History and Political Economy of Central America.* Boulder, Colo.: Westview Press, 1994.

———. "Reform and (Counter-)Revolution in Post-Independence Guatemala: Liberalism, Conservatism, and Postmodern Controversies." *Latin American Perspectives* 26 (1999): 129–158.

Wells, William V. *Explorations and Adventures in Honduras.* New York: Harper & Bros. 1857.

Werlich, David P. *Admiral of the Amazon: John Randolph Tucker, His Confederate Colleagues, and Peru.* Charlottesville: University of Virginia Press, 1990.

Woodward, Ralph Lee. *Central America: A Nation Divided.* 3rd ed. New York: Oxford University Press, 1999.

———. *Rafael Carrera and the Emergence of the Republic of Guatemala, 1821–1871.* Athens: University of Georgia Press, 1993.

Yankelevich, Pablo. *Honduras: Una breve historia.* México, D.F.: Instituto de Investigaciones Dr. José Maria Luis Mora, Universidad de Guadalajara, 1988.

Index

Page numbers in **bold** indicate
illustrations.